THE 60 MINUTE STARTUP

A PROVEN SYSTEM TO START YOUR BUSINESS IN ONE HOUR A DAY AND GET YOUR FIRST PAYING CUSTOMERS IN THIRTY DAYS (OR LESS)

RAMESH DONTHA

ISBN: 9781705797549
Imprint: Independently published

Printed in the United States of America

Table of Contents

To my late father Yadagiri Dontha and to my mother Suguna Dontha. I cherish your unconditional love and support.

To my wife Sunanda and to our daughters Megha and Nidhi. You have always motivated me by saying that my book will have at least three readers.

What's Next?

www.the60minutestartup.com

Start your business today the agile way! As a valued reader, you get all the templates, scripts, and tools you need to build your 60-minute startup, all at no cost to you.

Just visit this special web page for your free content upgrades so you can set up your business, build a website and other online assets, attract paying customers, and more in the shortest time possible.

www.the60minutestartup.com

Tell Me What You Think

Let other readers know what you thought of *The 60-Minute Startup*. Please write an honest review for this book on Amazon or on your favorite online bookshop.

Foreword

A friend of mine once solicited business startup advice from a stranger on a bus in San Francisco. The stranger looked like a hipster engineer, and my friend decided to "put herself out there" on the chance that he was someone who could introduce her to investors. He ended up asking her out and now they're married with a two year-old. But she never did get her business off the ground. (Success or failure? You decide.)

Before hitting up your cousin –the one with the baseball cap that says, "I roll my own"-- your ex-colleague with a room to rent in Silicon Beach, or that rideshare driver whose Prius smells like boiled meat, reach across the banquette for ***The 60 Minute Startup***. It can be your mentor – and it doesn't expect you to pick up the lunch tab.

I wish Ramesh's book was around when I started my firm. Why, you might be wondering, do I think you should add it to your library? Three reasons:

- ***The 60-Minute Startup*** is tactical. I love that Ramesh homes in on agility. What would you buy if you had a nickel for every entrepreneur who overthought her business plan? (Asking for a friend.) Ramesh introduces concepts of the agile framework, prescribing practical steps for propelling your company forward, not tinkering with spreadsheet-intensive revenue projections for

ephemeral investors. And while we're on that topic, do you even *need* investors? (Again, asking for a friend.) Ramesh includes actionable checklists that have been field-proven by entrepreneurs, many of whom are almost as smart as you!

- It's real-world. Yeah, in the real world the best founders are delivery-focused. They quit looking inward and down (*Should we re-run first-year sales projections before we agree to the meeting?)*, instead focusing outward (*That person fits our profile for the ideal prospect!*). Ramesh shares examples from other people's companies, so you can see—IRL!—how successful people consider their goals. Did I say I wish this book were around when I started my firm?
- It's about people. There's nothing like learning from other people who have done what we want to do, the right way. Ramesh knows some pros who have practiced what he preaches. In ***The 60-Minute Startup*** he introduces them, and they color in what success looks like. After reading their profiles, I'm proclaiming myself Dr. Gayle Carson's biggest fangirl, I want to help Melissa Celikel "Make SHT Happen," and I'm determined to "Be Like Kenzi."

Oh, and I'm recommending that you re-read ***The 60-Minute Startup*** every year. The world has changed since I started my company, and my answers to the book's assessment questions would be completely different

based on the skills and interests I've developed since then. ***The 60-Minute Startup*** guides you in how to differentiate yourself. Moreover, it leaves room for how you've evolved and what you have to offer today. (The answer is: A LOT!)

I launched my company after a few years of deliberation, which followed a few years of self-assessment, which followed a few years of unfulfilling work. I sold that company a few years ago, and it was a great run. I have few regrets. Still, we made our share of mistakes those first few years. At the end of each chapter, Ramesh asks us, "What did you learn about your business (or yourself) today that will serve you in the future?" Like I said, I wish his book had been there for us back then. But it's here now! And trust me, it will release your entrepreneurial mojo!

Plus, it's good practice in case a stranger on a bus asks what you're up to.

~ Jill Dyché, Author, *eData* and *The New IT*

September 2019

60

The Secret to Launching a Successful Business Faster Than You Ever Imagined

Sally and Sunder both want to start a business.

Sally spends weeks researching business ideas, potential products, and target markets. She's surrounded herself with so much information she's more lost than when she started. Sunder asks himself a simple question: "If I sell X, who will buy it and for how much?" He does his homework and finds the answer within the hour.

Sally takes a branding master class and plays with her logo, color palettes, and fonts until they're *perfect*. She changes her mind a month later and starts over from

scratch. Sunder spends a few minutes on a free online brand creator and calls it a day. His design won't win any awards, but it's good enough to make people take his business seriously.

Sally reads a book about asking customers what they want before building a product, so she invests in ads to push out her survey. Sally gets conflicting answers, so she runs the ad again. She throws her hands in the air and goes with her first gut instinct. Sunder reads the same book, but all he does is talk to a few people in his network, and he makes his first sale by the weekend.

Sally "starts with why," takes complex personal assessments, and creates a vision board. Sunder makes more sales.

Sally downloads ten free niche finder exercises but still has no idea what her niche should be. Sunder skipped that step yet he still has paying customers—the only niche that matters to new entrepreneurs.

Sally takes a free business plan writing course at her local small business development center. She finishes the class, changes her mind, and scraps the plan altogether. Sunder follows a simple, proven business plan to get and keep his first paying customers, and it works like a charm.

Sally subscribes to marketing "experts" and buys courses on funnels, email marketing, and social media. For the next three months, she makes no progress on her business—but she's learning a lot about marketing! Meanwhile, Sunder builds a bare minimum online presence and has enough repeat customers by this point to quit his nine-to-five job.

Sally's path is the one most new entrepreneurs follow. It's painstakingly slow, has a steep learning curve, and results in mixed success, if any. After several months, Sally hasn't made any sales and doesn't know what to do next. Not only has she failed in her business, but she's failed to even begin!

Sunder chose **agile entrepreneurship**—the new way to start a profitable business and get paying customers fast while everyone else is stuck and overwhelmed. It's rapid. It's flexible. It's *agile*.

How do you want to start your business? Do you want to be like Sally or Sunder? Every entrepreneur wants to start making money as soon as possible, whether they end up selling products or offering a service. So how do you do that? How do you start your own business in one hour a day and get your first paying customers in thirty days or less?

Let me show you how to be like Sunder.

The Wonderful World of Agile Entrepreneurship

Let's back up a second and see how *Merriam-Webster* defines the word "agile."

1. Marked by the ready ability to move with quick and easy grace
2. Having a quick, resourceful, and adaptable character

Typical startup founders invest years and fortunes building the structure of a business that may never produce a profit.

Agile entrepreneurs are different—they believe good enough to make money is good enough to make money.

I'll say that again.

Good enough to make money is good enough to make money.

Agile entrepreneurs believe in real-life feedback over business school theories. Fast over methodical. Done now over done well. Money in the bank over money spent on courses. You might say agile entrepreneurs are in it for the money, and rightly so. What's the point of starting a business if you never make money? Finding your true passion may or may not put food on your table. Yet I haven't found a single book that teaches you the essentials of starting a business and getting your first paying customers right away. That's why I decided to write one.

If you're agile, you get to revenue as fast as you can. How? You work on something small, execute it quickly, get feedback, and adapt your plan from there. This process of small, fast, and repeated cycles is known as "iterative." You see what works, what works better, and what doesn't work at all, change your behavior accordingly, rinse, and repeat.

If Sunders always beat Sallys, why haven't you learned about agile entrepreneurship before, right? Why aren't all the business books and courses teaching it? Agile isn't native to solopreneurs, one-hundred-dollar startups, or the gig economy. *Agility* is a word I've heard often in my career as a systems analyst, product manager, and a management consultant. Fortune 100 companies have sent me all over

India, Europe, and the United States to make information technology systems more efficient. I would like to take credit for the agile approach, but that credit goes to a team of software developers at a ski lodge in Utah's Wasatch Mountains.

In February 2001, seventeen developers[1] from around the world met for a three-day retreat to get drunk over problems with their bosses and share ideas on how to get projects done on time. This was a casual event. Little planning went into it beyond booking the lodge. Yet what emerged from their conversations was the Agile Software Development Manifesto. This profound document changed the way developers plan projects, collaborate with coworkers, report to management, and meet deadlines. The manifesto states four primary values[2] that should guide every project:

1. Individuals and interactions over processes and tools
2. Working software over comprehensive documentation
3. Customer collaboration over contract negotiation
4. Responding to change over following a plan

The agile approach revolutionized software, made Silicon Valley the tech capital of the world, and made possible the Airbnbs, Dropboxes, Instagrams, and Ubers we can't

---

[1] History: The Agile Manifesto. Accessed September 4, 2019. https://agilemanifesto.org/history.html.

[2] "Comprehensive Guide to the Agile Manifesto." Smartsheet. Accessed September 4, 2019. https://www.smartsheet.com/comprehensive-guide-values-principles-agile-manifesto.

imagine living without. If agile software founders can build companies worth billions in a garage, imagine what agile entrepreneurship can do for you! Well, you don't have to imagine—*you* can be the next Sunder. You don't have to get stuck at non-money-making stages like non-agile entrepreneurs do. You don't need to find the ideal business model, create a perfect value proposition, or design a beautiful marketing funnel. Not before you make your first sale, at least. When it comes to agile entrepreneurship, paying customers are first. Everything else is second.

How to Use This Book

60 minutes a day x 30 days = 1 viable business

That's my promise to you if you read and apply everything in the pages to come. As I wrote this book, I skipped all the typical (bad) startup advice and trimmed essential tasks down to the *most* essential. Ever heard of the 80/20 rule? Eighty percent of the results you want come from 20 percent of your effort. Well, *The 60-Minute Startup* is more like a 99/1 rule. That means you're doing one thing here and one thing there that have a big impact. Since leaving my corporate job, I've founded three profitable companies. I can tell you from experience that what *feels* productive often isn't. The only truly important activities to start and build a business aren't the ones that take days and weeks to finish. In fact, they don't take as long as you might expect. Only a few tasks lead to sales. For aspiring entrepreneurs like you, that is your only goal. Sales. No sales means no business.

This book is meant to be read one chapter a day for thirty consecutive days. In each chapter, I'll show you what to do next and how to get it done fast. Each chapter opens with a story of a successful entrepreneur who took the agile approach to that day's activities. That way, you can see for yourself what that task looks like when it's done right. You'll also see a checklist of steps for the day, suggested time for each, and any templates you need to get the day's work done in sixty minutes or less. If you read one chapter every day and complete the tasks, you *will* have paying customers in thirty days. For any tech tasks that change over time (e.g., building your website), I'll direct you to www.The60MinuteStartup.com for my most up-to-date resources. That way you can start your own business today, whether you're reading this book in 2019, 2029, or beyond!

Over the next thirty days, we're going to borrow principles from the Agile Software Development Manifesto and apply them to your entrepreneurial dream. We'll do so using something called a *scrum*. Our scrum is the recipe we'll follow, which tells us what essential ingredients we need for our agile framework. Agile is the *what*, and *scrum* is the how. Let's break down the critical elements of our scrum:

- Sprint
- Sprint team
- Product backlog

- Sprint backlog
- Story points
- Sprint planning
- Daily standup
- Sprint review
- Sprint retro

In a scrum, you **sprint** to get meaningful work accomplished over a defined time period. In *The 60-Minute Startup*, we'll have four sprints that are each a week long (so we'll finish in thirty days or less).

A **sprint team** comprises the owner, the scrum master (a servant-leader who manages and coaches the team while tracking deliverables), and anyone else working on the scrum. In our case, the owner is you, the scrum master is me, and the rest of the team is anyone who helps you accomplish the day's task or the week's sprint (a web developer, a content writer, an attorney, etc.). You're taking a team approach to everything you do. You're not in this alone. In every chapter, you're going to witness how another agile entrepreneur accomplished the same tasks you're going to do that day. You're essentially joining a sprint team of superstars. That way you'll start (and finish) each day feeling motivated to keep going!

The **product backlog** is simply a list of the requirements needed to develop a meaningful product. In our case, the product backlog is the list of all the tasks you'll accomplish in this book over the next thirty days to start your business and get paying customers. You're prioritizing the important things. Your only objective right now is to get your first paying customers. Prioritize every task that gets you closer to that goal. For example, would designing a website get you a paying customer? One of the businesses I own now is a management consulting firm, where we help big companies make better decisions using big data. The majority of our customers find us with a Google search. For that business, I prioritized a website because having one is critical to us getting customers. For other businesses, a social media profile page would be sufficient, so the website can wait. When you start a business, figuring out what to do and in what order is one of the hardest things to do. That's why I've defined what the highest priority actions are and laid them out for you in the order you should do them.

The **sprint backlog** is the list of things that need to be accomplished during each sprint. In our case, the first week's sprint is all about your product or service and its viability. The second sprint is all about forming a legally recognized company and setting up minimum viable operations. Week three's sprint has you finding and attracting potential customers. During the fourth and final sprint, you'll convert prospects into customers, make repeat sales, and get your first referrals. Congratulations! You now have a business.

Story points are essentially a breakdown of each task into steps with how long it takes to do each step. Don't worry about being exact. An estimate is good enough. Knowing what you know now, what kind of turnaround can you expect on this step? You make an initial estimate of how much effort you'll need to put into a task, then you keep updating that estimate based on how things are going. Every day I estimate that the tasks I give you in each chapter will take sixty minutes. If one day's tasks go quicker, feel free to take on the next chapter and dive in if you have the time. If another day's tasks end up taking you two hours, extend that chapter's work into the next day. It all evens out in the end. Flexibility is part of the agile approach.

When you're **sprint planning**, you're figuring out what input needs to go into a particular sprint. Don't worry—I've already made these decisions for you. Your sixty-minute task list for every day for the next thirty days is done and waiting for you.

The **daily standup** is a self-assessment. Every day during a software project, team members keep each other accountable by asking each other short questions like "What did you get done today? How are you doing since yesterday? What do you need to carry over to work on tomorrow?" At the end of each day (chapter), you'll see this simple multiple-choice standup, and you'll check the appropriate box:

- ❏ I got today's tasks done early, so I'm going to get a head start on tomorrow.
- ❏ I got everything done today in about sixty minutes.
- ❏ I need to come back and do ______________ tomorrow.

Will you need to check the first or third box often? It's doubtful. Your task list for each day includes only the essential activities that lead to your first, second, third (and so on) paying customers.

A **sprint review** is exactly what it sounds like. At the end of each week, you review what you've accomplished. In *The 60-Minute Startup*, I'll give you the opportunity to review what you got done each week and prepare for what's next.

In a **sprint retro**, you ask yourself how you can improve. What did you learn during the last sprint that you can apply in the future? I provide a space for you to answer this question after each week for your sprint retros.

I have a unique perspective on the agile approach because I used it as a product manager, consultant, and entrepreneur. Before agile methodology, software development was tedious. We got detailed project requirements from the client in months one and two. We didn't start developing the product until the third month. Yet everybody knew the requirements would change. So when change occurred—priorities shifted, key personnel quit, economy crashed, et cetera—the first two months were wasted. When we took the agile approach, we went straight to prototyping in the first month. I'd show our client the first prototype of their user interface and logo, and they'd either say, "Yes, perfect," or "No, that's not what I meant." If they didn't like it, we went back to the drawing board. Either way, we lost no time.

This approach applies to all entrepreneurial journeys. When you draw up a business plan, it's never perfect, right? It's going to change because change happens. Not everything you write down on day one is going to stick. So you keep evolving that business plan. If you have a general idea about what you're going to do, that's good enough. Go do it, see what happens, and adjust your next steps.

Jason Patel is a perfect example. If you listened to his interview on *The Agile Entrepreneur Podcast*, you know his story. Jason is a college and career prep consultant who built his business the agile way. When he started his business, he thought his clientele would be colleges and government organizations. Jason would get them to buy into his consulting, then they'd send students and professionals to him who needed his help. That didn't work out the way he'd expected. So Jason pivoted his business to work with students and their parents one on one, which led to his first sales.

Another entrepreneur I know—Janet Elie—trains small business owners in search engine optimization (SEO). It's a different model from her competition. She's not offering done-for-you SEO; she's training business owners and their teams to do it themselves. The first idea Janet came up with was SEO services for insurance agents. When that didn't work out, she evolved her business to her current offer.

For both entrepreneurs, the agile approach drove success. They didn't waste undue time and effort on a service they didn't know if people wanted or not. They tested it, took the feedback, and tried something new. It's like the prototyping I did as a product developer. I've heard so many entrepreneurs say, "I need to have the perfect product before I do anything." That's a sure way to fail like Sally. Put your product or service out there, perfect or not, so you can get feedback and make changes as necessary. Even before I permanently left my corporate job in 2016, I started a few businesses as a side hustle. The first one was a website, www.ChoicePetMeds.com, which I bought, grew, and sold for a profit. The website was essentially a pet medicine retail store where I earned commissions from the website sales.

Why did I buy a business rather than building one? I wanted paying customers from day one. When I bought the website, it was already optimized to rank high in internet search results. Product and prescription fulfillment was already set up, so I was the middleman who didn't need to worry about inventory.

Even though my site was successful from the beginning, I didn't know how to scale the business to get more customers. So I followed the agile way. Remember the second agile concept? *Setting priorities*. Getting more customers was my number one priority, so I focused all my efforts on marketing. I was willing to fail fast and fail often, which meant I won more often than I lost. For example, I wrote pet care and pet medicine blog articles to build interest in my products and rank even higher in search results. Some articles worked; some didn't. The overall result? More customers.

Alongside the pet pharmacy website, I got into the business of buying and selling domain names. At one point, I owned over eight hundred domains. I worked on one of them at a time. I'd build a website, develop an email capture system to market to subscribers, and write sales pages to convert those subscribers into buyers. Then I'd sell the website for a profit to someone who wanted to take it to the next level like I did with www.ChoicePetMeds.com. Of course, not every domain was profitable, but the net result was that I learned to build businesses the agile way by tinkering with the business model.

Fast forward to today, and I follow the agile approach with every new entrepreneurial venture. I prototype, prove it works, tweak what doesn't, and evolve in the direction of getting customers. I'm going to teach you how to do the same, whether you're starting your first business or your next one. In just one hour a day, you will:

- Identify what you bring to your industry that no one else does.
- Never waste a minute on menial tasks that don't lead to customers.
- Set up your business right so that you never have to worry about the government auditing you.
- Create a simple "know your numbers" system so you'll know when and how much to outsource.

- Get clear on what people will pay you for and how much.
- Master branding essentials so that prospects take you seriously—even before your first sale.
- Build a website that generates leads so that you wake up to an inbox full of inquiries.
- Learn (and ask) the one question that gets people begging to buy from you.
- Do only things that lead directly to sales.
- Pay yourself first and well.
- Write a simple business plan so that you achieve your goals on autopilot.
- Know exactly what you're supposed to do each day.
- Get your first paying customers even if you don't know your "why" or your niche.
- Market your business like a growth hacker even if you hate marketing.
- Turn chance conversations into instant sales without feeling salesy.
- Build a pipeline of leads so that you have more than enough potential clients to make your business work.
- Respect yourself so that you never have to take on clients that make you bitter.
- Make sales without feeling awkward or getting haggled on price.

- Have your own business up, running, and profitable one month from today.

Really, Ramesh? All that in thirty days? You're probably thinking to yourself. Yes, every outcome I list is not only possible but also *likely* when you build your business the agile way. In the coming pages, I'm going to introduce you to thirty agile entrepreneurs who started their businesses in record time. While aspiring entrepreneur friends sat around brainstorming business names, these entrepreneurs made sales and got referrals. Don't waste another minute on articles, emails, podcasts, tutorials, and lengthy business books that get you trapped in busywork. If you want to make money now, the agile way is the only way for you.

"But Ramesh, What If . . . ?"

With a promise like mine (paying customers in one hour a day in just thirty days), you might still have your doubts. I would if I were you! I bet you're thinking, *This agile business thing seems all well and good, but what if it doesn't work for me? I don't have any business experience.*

Fair question. The entire point of *The 60-Minute Startup* is that you don't *need* any business experience. All the experience you need—knowing what to do and when to do it—comes with this book. You don't have to figure out *anything* by yourself. You're following in the footsteps of successful entrepreneurs who've built thriving businesses the agile way. So the question isn't "Will this work for me?" it's "Can I follow instructions?" If you can, you have nothing to worry about. This book can and will work for you.

But Ramesh, what if I can't get everything done in just one hour a day? Won't it take like seven days to build my website, set up my social media, and write my marketing emails? Not with *The 60-Minute Startup* it won't. Every day, I give you what you need to get your tasks done. For example, when it's time to write your emails to reach out to prospects, I give you my templates. I've already tested these templates, so all you have to do is copy, paste, modify as necessary, and send. The same goes with every other complex task. Even web design. The hard work is already done for you. If you can download a template, you can start your own business and get paying customers in thirty days or less.

Still worried you're the exception? That the agile approach I teach may not work in your industry, with your idea, or for you personally? *The 60-Minute Startup* is for serious entrepreneurs who want a real business with real customers as soon as possible. Now, not every business model allows that. For example, if you're starting a fitness center, you need capital, equipment, and employees. You can expect many months and lots of money to go into that business before you sign up your first member. I could not pass the red-face test and promise you sales in thirty days. But if your dream is to open a fitness center, why not start a personal fitness coaching business? You won't need a lot of upfront commitment to start your agile business. After you use this book to get your paying customers in thirty days, then you can work on opening your fitness center. First things first. It's the agile way.

No matter your industry, idea, or personality, all you need to get started is this book, a computer, and an internet connection. A dedicated space such as a home office or a comfortable garage helps, but it's optional. If the laptop lifestyle appeals to you, you can build your own business from anywhere.

Did you know that 70 percent[3] of people want to start a business, but less than 15 percent[4] of aspiring entrepreneurs go from idea to ownership? My goal is to close this entrepreneurship desire gap and make you one of the few who starts, builds, and grows a viable, profitable business.

Let's begin!

---

[3] Reid, Susan. "The Numbers Are In: Most People Want To Be Their Own Boss." Forbes. *Forbes Magazine*, January 8, 2016. https://www.forbes.com/sites/susanreid/2015/10/12/the-numbers-are-in-most-people-want-to-be-their-own-boss/#3517b2ae1451.

[4] Buchanan, Leigh. "The U.S. Now Has 27 Million Entrepreneurs." Inc.com. *Inc.*, September 2, 2015. https://www.inc.com/leigh-buchanan/us-entrepreneurship-reaches-record-highs.html.

Day 1: Don't Start with Why, Start with What

The Accidental Entrepreneur

Paige Arnof-Fenn is the founder and CEO of the global marketing and branding firm Mavens and Moguls based in Cambridge, Massachusetts. For eighteen years, Paige has built her company into a market leader. Her clients include Microsoft, Virgin, *The New York Times*, Colgate, venture capitalist–backed startups, and nonprofit organizations. Her marketing advice has graced the pages of *Entrepreneur* and *Forbes*.

Paige calls herself an accidental entrepreneur. In her early career, she worked in marketing at global companies like Procter & Gamble and Coca-Cola. She assumed that was the path she would follow forever. She credits a couple of incidents for giving her the opportunity to start her own business. The first was the invention of the internet, which gave her an opportunity to hone her craft doing marketing and brand development virtually for tech startups. The second was the economic depression after the September 11, 2001, World Trade Center tragedy. The aftermath opened a void in marketing services that no company filled. That gap inspired Paige to start her own company. But what kind of a company? Let's rewind Paige's story a bit.

Back when Paige was a student at Stanford University, then Harvard Business School, she dreamed of becoming the next Meg Whitman, Ursula Burns, or Carly Fiorina. She saw herself one day running a multinational company. Then Paige became intrigued by what was happening with technology online. So she joined her first startup as the head of marketing, raising tens of millions of dollars and riding the dot-com wave. They went public and were sold to Yahoo.

Paige felt motivated and energized working in a start-up environment. Things were a lot scrappier. She didn't have the safety net or big budget she had at Coca-Cola. Even though her company raised a lot of money, the budgets ran tight. Paige learned to be effective at "guerilla marketing" in a way established, well-funded brands never have to. Exciting times!

Then Paige's husband got a job in Boston, and they moved to the East Coast. There she joined a second startup as the head of marketing. Then a third startup. The internet continued its boom. All three of Paige's companies reached profitability and positive exits selling to large corporations. While working at these startups, Paige learned how much she loved the idea of helping create what could be the next great brand.

Around the time the third startup was sold, September 11 happened. Beyond the tragedy of lives lost, the event jolted the economy, impacting marketing intensely. Money was difficult to raise. Companies shut down marketing departments to conserve their cash.

Paige had a lot of good contacts in the venture world, and a lot of them asked her for help post–September 11. She already knew a lot of other people who were great at marketing and looking for work. She saw an opportunity. She knew the people, she knew the projects, she had the network—and the timing was perfect for her to connect the dots. So, slowly, she started putting people together with projects. Before she knew it, her new business was off and running. It's not where she thought she was headed, but eighteen years later, she's still having a lot of fun.

Paige never wrote a business plan before she started her company. She worked hard over the years to build her reputation, develop contacts, and grow a strong network.

Her experience, training, skill set, and network aligned with the opportunity in the market.

The first year, Paige hustled. She networked, knocked on doors, and gave a lot of talks. Her hard work paid off—from year one to year two, Mavens and Moguls *quadrupled* in revenue. Year two to year three, they tripled. By the third year she had great references and testimonials. She started getting a lot of referrals and repeat clients. Even though she had paying customers from the get-go and was growing steadily in the first two years, the third year was the breakout year for Paige. Her alma mater Harvard Business School published a few case studies on her company, Mavens and Moguls. They became a model of success—a woman-owned entrepreneurial business in the service sector that could scale. That's when they gained market validation. And it never even dawned on Paige that she might fail. She just knew she would be successful. She worked hard with great people.

There's one key that Paige credits her firm's success to—she always screens her customers. This way she rarely ends up with "bad clients." She helps each of her customers based on their specific needs, as opposed to one size fits all. And she's not afraid to fire customers if they're not a good match for her firm.

Mavens and Moguls helps establish and build brands, create logos and taglines, and develop marketing materials. Paige feels that great marketing can help all kinds of businesses get their stories straight and find their audience.

Paige also believes in the importance of customer research, market research, market validation, and adjusting one's plans based on actual data rather than on opinions. Sound complicated? Don't worry—I'm going to help you do all the necessary research in your one hour a day.

What Do You Bring to the Party?

According to Peter Drucker, the father of business and management consulting, a business has only one purpose: to create a customer. A customer is anyone who pays a business for goods and services. Mr. Drucker goes on to say that creating a customer has two basic functions: marketing and innovation. So the key question for you as an entrepreneur is "What do you bring to the party to make marketing and innovation to create a customer who pays you?" Unfortunately, most of the conventional wisdom and advice tells entrepreneurs like you to start with "Why?" But why does the customer care if the reason for starting your business is that you got laid off or you want a flexible schedule?

To have a paying customer for your goods and services, let's start thinking about these fundamental questions (no need to take notes yet—that will come at the end of this chapter):

- What knowledge, skills, abilities, and assets do you bring to your business to make marketing and innovation happen?
- What problems are you planning to solve for your customers?

- What products and services will you offer to your target customers?
- What benefits will your products/services offer to the customer that they'll be willing to pay for?

Starting today, we'll find the answers to these fundamental questions. Today's focus is on discovering what you bring to the party. Notice how we're not "starting with why," a popular entrepreneurship proverb that has you come up with a business idea based on what is meaningful to you. In my experience starting, growing, and selling businesses, what is most important to you doesn't always match a problem or need that people will pay you for. So why not start with what your future customers want from you?

When Paige started her business, she knew she was bringing her extensive experience in marketing and branding for technology startups, her vast network that she'd built over the years, and the money she had put aside.

According to research,[5] people who start businesses based on their knowledge and skills are more likely to succeed than those who chase a trend or pursue a "passion" but have no corresponding strength. If you're passionate about the areas where you have extensive experience and a strong skill set, your business has a higher probability of success in the long term. Paige is passionate about marketing and branding, and that's where her strengths lie. That's why

[5] https://fortune.com/2014/09/25/why-startups-fail-according-to-their-founders/

she's been able to run her business successfully for eighteen years and counting.

We're going to list all your knowledge, skills, abilities, and assets to get you started. The advantage of putting them on paper now is you can always come back to them as you iterate through your business plans. Most businesses evolve over time. As you learn more about yourself and your customers, you may tweak your business.

Before we start listing them, let's get clear on what exactly knowledge, skills, abilities, and assets are.

What Is Knowledge?

Knowledge focuses on the understanding of concepts. It is theoretical and not practical. An individual may have an understanding of a topic or tool but have no experience applying it. For example, someone might have read hundreds of articles on health and nutrition, many of them in scientific journals, but that doesn't make that person qualified to dispense advice on nutrition.

What Are Skills?

Skills are the capabilities developed through training or hands-on experience. Skills are the practical application of knowledge. Someone can take a course on investing and gain knowledge of it. But only experience in trading gives them the skills.

What Are Abilities?

Abilities, often confused with skills, are the innate traits or talents that you bring to a task or situation. Many people can learn to negotiate competently by acquiring knowledge and practicing skills. But a few are brilliant negotiators because they have an innate ability to persuade.

What Are Assets?

Assets are funds you have saved up or that you acquire through loans, investors, or fund-raising. So how do assets work with everything else to push your business from idea into reality? Take a look at the example below. This is what I call the knowledge, skills, abilities, and assets matrix:

Category	Example	Level of Competency (1 for expert, 2 for intermediate, 3 for basic)	Level of Personal Passion/ Interest (1 for passionate, 2 for enjoy, 3 for moderate interest)	Customers Who Can Benefit
Knowledge				
Design and execute marketing campaigns	Developed Microsoft Windows marketing plan	1	2	Marketing departments of medium-to-large businesses Marketing agencies Small business owners
Develop brands for companies	Developed Virgin Music brand	2	1	Marketing departments of medium-to-large businesses Marketing agencies

Skills				
Copywriting	Microsoft and Virgin advertisement copy	1	2	Marketing agencies
Public speaking	Tech Accelerator conference	2	1	Conference organizers
Abilities				
Develop completely new ideas	Conceptualized Virgin Music brand from scratch	1	1	Marketing departments of medium-to-large businesses Marketing agencies Small business owners
Manage multiple projects simultane-ously	Handled three account launches at the same time	2	1	Marketing departments of medium-to-large businesses Marketing agencies Small business owners
Assets				
	$30,000 (personal finances)	N/A	N/A	N/A
	$20,000 (loan)	N/A	N/A	N/A
	Core network of 100 people	N/A	N/A	N/A
	Extended network of 1,000 contacts	N/A	N/A	N/A

Your Inventory: Now It's Your Turn

Check off the box beside each task as you complete it.

❑ **1. Complete knowledge, skills, abilities, assets matrix: 30 minutes**

Download the blank template for the matrix at www.The60MinuteStartup.com. For this and for all future templates, you can print it out and handwrite, or you can keep it saved on your computer and type into the fields. Whichever you choose, just make sure you keep all your materials in one place so that they're easy to come back to.

In the first column, list three to five items each for knowledge, skills, abilities, and assets in the matrix template.

❑ **2. Prioritize your competency and interest: 15 minutes**

In the second column of the matrix, assign a level of competency and confidence to each item. In the third column, assign a level of passion and interest to each item.

❑ **3. Identify your potential customers: 15 minutes**

In the fourth column, identify potential customers who could benefit from each of the rows in your knowledge, skills, and abilities sections.

Daily Standup

Did you complete today's tasks?

- ❑ Yes
- ❑ No

If no, what do you need to carry over to work on tomorrow?

____

What did you learn about your business (or yourself) today that will serve you in the future?

____

Day 2: Creating Customers

A Jill of All Trades Who Never Stops Selling

Dr. Gayle Carson refers to herself as "a spunky old broad." She's started many successful businesses over the years, including a modeling school and a talent agency. Today, she's a best-selling author and in-demand public speaker. She runs SpunkyOldBroad.com and SOBRadioNetwork.com.

Gayle's customer philosophy is that if you don't have ready-to-pay customers in your pipeline, your business will die. And from day one as an entrepreneur, Gayle found customers willing to pay. As a model, she realized she had a knack for teaching others, so she used that natural ability to start her modeling school. When that took off, she knew she'd have a customer base to start and run a talent agency. . . so that's just what she did.

As both businesses grew, Gayle saw a new opportunity to provide convention services (coordinating services for groups holding events). That grew into a multisite business venture, employing hundreds of people. Despite such massive professional success, Gayle has faced personal life-shattering hardships. She's lost both her son and husband and has gone through chemotherapy for cancer treatment. Nevertheless, Gayle remains an eternal optimist. Even though she's over eighty, Gayle spends hours every week doing radio shows. What does she spend all that time talking about? How women over fifty can start their own businesses. Age is nothing but a number. She's seen it firsthand—the opportunity for paying customers is all around you no matter how old (or young) you are. You just have to find them.

Paying Customers: The Only Niche That Matters

"Find your niche." Heard that advice before? We all have. After you find a niche of customers, you're supposed to find a subniche to have even less competition selling your product or service. When I started my data strategy company, I tried that. It took me months to research different niches and validate business ideas in each one. At the end of it, all I had was frustration. I had no idea which niche to pick, and I'd wasted valuable time I could've used to find paying customers instead. That's when I realized the only niche that matters is the one with customers who are ready to pay.

Gayle's ability to find ready-to-pay customers was the key to her setting up successful business after successful business. She created customers, nurtured their relationships, and kept providing value.

To create a paying customer, you've got to know what their pain points are. With this knowledge, you can offer a solution that solves those pain points that they're willing to pay for. So, what exactly is a pain point? It's a specific problem your prospective customers are dealing with. Pain points can be diverse and complex depending on who your prospective customers are, but they all fall into four main categories:

- Financial Pain Points: Your customers are having cash flow problems. This could be due to high expenses, business growth, or lack of a customer pipeline.
- Productivity Pain Points: Your prospects aren't using their time well. They could do a better job developing new offers, improving their daily operations, or running their households.
- Process Pain Points: Your customers' processes are sloppy and need improvement. This improvement could look like finding a quicker, easier way to complete a frustrating task.

- Support Pain Points: Your customer isn't getting the support they need when they need it. Think both emotional support (e.g., words of encouragement) and practical support (e.g., a done-for-you service).

Today we'll define the pain points of your potential customers and find solutions they're willing to pay for, thereby creating your very own ideal customer. Taking your list from Day 1, you're going to complete a spreadsheet like the one below. Visit www.The60MinuteStartup.com for a downloadable template.

Customer	Pain Points	Your Potential Offering
Marketing agency		
Marketing department of medium company		
Solopreneurs		
Small business owners		

Create a Customer: Now It's Your Turn

Check off the box beside each task as you complete it.

❑ **1. Copy the customers list from Day 1 into the template: 5 minutes**

On Day 1, you wrote down a list of your assets and the potential customers who could benefit from them. Copy the list of customers into the template below.

Customer	Pain Points	Your Potential Offering

- [ ] **2. Identify their pain points: 40 minutes**

  For each potential customer, write down three to five pain points. Don't try to brainstorm too many. Then it'll be hard to figure out which one to solve! Aim for a dozen or so pain points total.

- [ ] **3. Write down products/services you can offer: 15 minutes**

  Write down a product/service you can offer to sell for each of the pain points. Keep in mind the expertise and assets you have at your disposal, which you wrote down on Day 1.

Daily Standup

Did you complete today's tasks?

- [ ] Yes
- [ ] No

If no, what do you need to carry over to work on tomorrow?

____

What did you learn about your business (or yourself) today that will serve you in the future?

____

Day 3: Selling What People Want to Buy

How This Freelance Blogger Came Up with a Successful Offer

Kenzi Wood worked full time in marketing. But she wanted flexibility. Freedom. She was tired of answering to somebody else. So Kenzi started writing content for company blogs on the side. Not only did writing come naturally to her—she enjoyed it! At first Kenzi charged companies ten cents a word for her content, but she quickly realized her rates were too low. She delivered value, and she deserved to get paid for it.

Initially Kenzi wasn't sure what specific area (niche) she should focus on. Because of her experience working with marketing agencies, Kenzi knew these agencies regularly needed compelling content for their clients. So she focused her offering on serving marketing agencies. Kenzi also offers a "jump-start" package where clients DIY their content as she coaches them. To grow her business, Kenzi asks every client for a testimonial and for referrals.

As a former marketer turned blogger, Kenzi now writes content for marketing agencies, SEO agencies, and Fortune 200 enterprises, as well as small mom-and-pop shops. With content designed to win, she stamps out flimsy copy—one blog at a time. Her mission is to increase reader engagement, website conversions, audience retention, and best of all, the business bottom line.

Be Like Kenzi

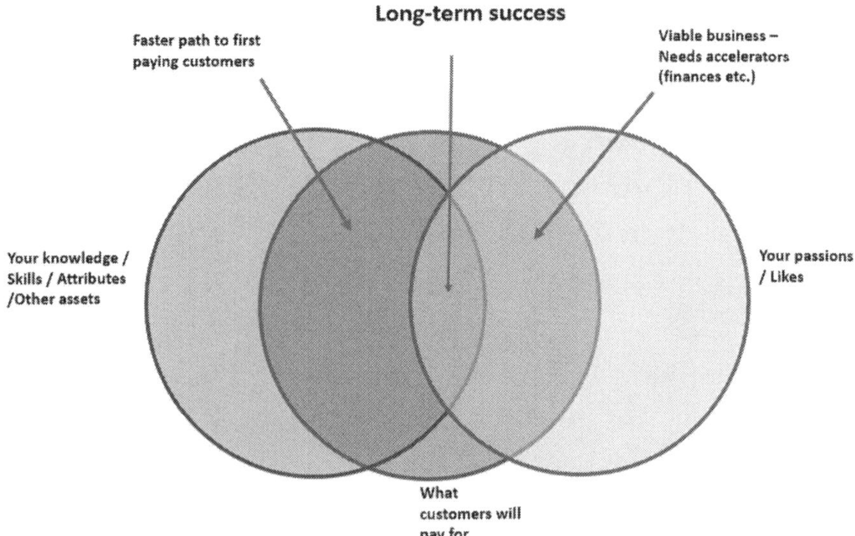

On Days 1 and 2, we established what you know (left circle) and what customers will pay for (middle circle). Let's keep building the spreadsheet we started on Day 1, focusing on these left and middle circles.

The circle on the right is the last piece of the puzzle for long-term business success. It's an important ingredient but not a critical one. You can build a viable, profitable business without passion. I've owned many purely money-making websites, one of which was a directory of websites for websites. Back in the days when Google valued backlinks from anywhere, website owners paid to get listed in my directories. Was I passionate about these directories? Not really. But I was able to get paying customers quickly because I knew about them.

Kenzi is a perfect example of using existing knowledge, skills, and attributes to build a new business. She has prior work experience with large companies and agencies, and she uses that knowledge and her skills to help small-to-medium-size companies market their businesses online.

Be like Kenzi—bring an aspect of what you already do into your new enterprise. Today's exercise is about finding the match between what you know and what customers are willing to pay for. That's how we'll come up with your product or service to get you paying customers.

Now, pull out your spreadsheet from the Day 2 exercise. Let's complete the remaining areas today. Use the spreadsheet from Day 1 to fill in column 5.

Customer	Pain Point	Product/ Service	Product/ Service Feature	Your Expertise That Will Make This Happen	Notes
Marketing Agencies	Need content to service their clients	Blog-writing service	500- to 1,000-word blog article	Content expertise on marketing topics	I am not an expert on graphics. May need to outsource if clients ask for a complete package.
Small or Medium Business Owner	Need content for their own blogs	Blog-writing service	500- to 1,000-word blog article	Writing skills	
Marketing Agencies	Need content to service their clients	Guest posting		Contacts with marketing agencies	Who'll provide websites for guest posting?

A Successful Offer: Now It's Your Turn

Check off the box beside each task as you complete it.

❑ **1. Complete columns 3 and 4 (product/service, product/service feature, notes): 30 minutes**

Here are some questions to ask yourself to help you fill out each column. Let's start with your customer's viewpoint:

- What exactly are you selling? Describe your product in terms of what it does for the customer.
- What does your product achieve, prevent, or preserve for the customer?

- How does the product improve your customer's life or work?
- What kind of customers will you be selling your product to? Describe your ideal customer.
- What price will you have to charge for your product for it to be profitable? Is there a real demand for your product at that price? (See Day 2 exercise.)
- Is the demand large enough for you to make a profit?
- Is the demand concentrated enough that you can advertise, sell, and deliver your product at a reasonable expense?

Dig deeper into the potential success of your product or service with the following critical questions:

- Who's going to sell the product?
- How is the product to be sold? What method of sales or process of promotion will you use?
- How is the product or service going to be manufactured or produced?
- How will you deliver your product to the customer?
- How will your product be serviced, repaired, guaranteed, or replaced?

Almost done! Before you make a final decision on your new product or service offering, ask these additional questions:

- Is there a real need for your product or service in today's market?
- What about your new product or service is better than what's currently available? Is your product lower priced or of better quality?
- What are three ways that your product is superior to its competition?
- Do you think you could become the number one supplier in the market for this product or service?

❑ **2. Complete column 5 (your expertise that can make this idea happen): 15 minutes**

Use information from Day 1's spreadsheet to complete what expertise you have or the asset you have to make this product/service feature happen.

❑ **3. Prioritize the product/service features: 15 minutes**

Now, look at all the features in your product/service feature column. Prioritize the ones that are most important. Pick five to ten features that are the most valuable to your customers. Don't stress over getting it perfect. Spend about fifteen minutes prioritizing your features.

Daily Standup

Did you complete today's tasks?

❑ Yes

❑ No

If no, what do you need to carry over to work on tomorrow?

____

What did you learn about your business (or yourself) today that will serve you in the future?

____

Day 4: Find Your Unique Value Proposition

Shirag Knows Best

Dr. Shirag Shemmassian wanted to attend one of the best colleges in the United States of America. The son of immigrant parents from Lebanon, Shirag originally set out to become a physician. He taught himself the skills needed to ace admissions exams and enrolled at Cornell University, a prestigious Ivy League school. After completing premedical requirements and receiving his undergraduate degree, Shirag decided to study mental health given his research interests and personal experiences with Tourette's syndrome, a disorder he was diagnosed with during childhood. Therefore, he earned his PhD in clinical psychology at UCLA.

Throughout Shirag's academic journey, fellow students approached him for help with gaining admission to top colleges, medical schools, and other graduate programs. *Sure, why not?* Shirag thought. So he helped them. Free of charge. Through word-of-mouth recommendations, more and more students approached Shirag for help. Could there be a real business opportunity here? The entrepreneur bug bit Shirag, and he never "recovered." In 2014, Dr. Shemmassian started an admissions consulting business as a side hustle. A little over five years later, he grew his business to seven-figure annual revenue.

Shirag's business, Shemmassian Academic Consulting, is a perfect example of the sweet spot of "what you know best," "what you like best," and "what customers are willing to pay for." Shirag's lack of business degree and business experience didn't deter him. He learned by trial and error. First, he had to figure out what to charge for his services. Based on his first few students' stellar admissions results, Shirag realized that what he delivered was much more valuable than what he was pricing it at—free.

Shirag started charging students, and his business grew. It grew so fast, in fact, that Shirag needed to hire other coaches to support his efforts as well as hire out other duties like accounting and marketing. Outsourcing these latter tasks was relatively easy, given that he didn't have complex processes. All he had to do was hire the best employees he could find. The real challenge was hiring other coaches who were just as capable as Shirag so he could protect the high standards that his own coaching had set. Through rigorous screening and training, Shirag found people he could trust. His business evolved, and his revenue increased.

What Differentiates You from Others?

As Dr. Shirag Shemmassian scaled his business from solo to a small team, he had to understand the unique value proposition (UVP) of his business. When you start taking on operations expenses like Shirag did, you can't risk a competitor coming along and out-marketing you. Shirag wanted to differentiate his business from similar businesses so he could continue growing profitably. How is a UVP the best way to do that? A UVP is a promise of unique value that your business delivers. The UVP at ridesharing app Uber is "the smartest way to get around." The Apple iPhone UVP is not any single feature but "the experience." Because "experience *is* the product."

Makes sense, right? Yet you're probably wondering why a UVP is critical for getting your first paying customer. As you read in earlier chapters, your knowledge, skills, and experience will help you get your product or service out the door. For the customer to pay *you* for your product or service, they must be convinced that your product or service will solve their problems better than similar offerings. Think lower price, more features, faster delivery, personalized support, or some other aspect that is *unique* compared to what you get from other businesses. Is your head spinning as you try to figure out what's unique about your business? I'll bet. So how do you come up with a unique value proposition for your business? Well, a UVP has three main components:

1. A specific customer demographic
2. A problem or need that you plan to address with your product or service
3. A benefit or solution for that problem or need

You can work with a few templates to brainstorm your UVP. I'm including a couple of examples for you below, but you can find a comprehensive list at www.The60MinuteStartup.com.

UVP Template 1

- For [target customer] who [statement of the need or opportunity], our [product/service name] is [product category] that [statement of benefit].
- Example: "For high school students who want to improve their academic test scores, our academic coaching service is one-on-one coaching that enables them to increase their grades by 20 percent."

UVP Template 2

- Customer: [who your target audience is] Problem: [what problem you're solving for the customer] Solution: [what is your solution to the problem]

- Example: "My best customers are high school students who are scoring in the 50th to 70th percentile without the coaching they need. My coaching services will increase their grades by at least 20 percent.

UVP Template 3

- Problem, Solution.
- Example: You're unable to increase your test scores beyond 5 percent on your own. I offer one-on-one coaching and specialized test-taking techniques to help you master difficult subject areas.

UVP Add-Ons

Here are some incremental value-adds you can consider that help you describe your product or service's uniqueness:

- Free shipping
- Next-day shipping
- Free bonus with purchase
- No setup fee
- No long-term contract, cancel any time
- Money-back guarantee
- Discounted price
- Customizable

Unique Value Proposition: Now It's Your Turn

Check off the box beside each task as you complete it.

❑ **1. Fine-tune your target customers: 20 minutes**

On Day 2, you identified your target customers. Now it's time to drill down into subsegments and look at those customers' specific problems and needs. This isn't niching down so much as getting clarity. For example, if you identified high school students as your target customers on Day 2, you might decide you want to target students seeking science degrees as your initial customers. Perhaps a better segment is the general population of students who live in your city. It's your call. What are their specific problems? Do they need coaching to improve their school grades or test scores? Do they need help with overall college prep or just test scores? Pick a specific demographic within your target market to start with.

❑ **2. Fine-tune the benefits of your offering: 20 minutes**

Drill down into the specific benefits your solution offers. Is it a lower price compared to the competition? Is yours delivered face-to-face as opposed to remotely? Do you offer unlimited practice or revisions? Find a unique angle to solve customers' specific problems in ways that are above and beyond your competition.

❑ **3. Put them all together: 20 minutes**

Put the outputs of steps 1 and 2 above into one single value proposition. See if you have identified a unique angle for your value proposition. If nothing comes to mind right away, play with the three templates above and the value-adds until you come up with a UVP you feel proud of.

Daily Standup

Did you complete today's tasks?

- ❑ Yes
- ❑ No

If no, what do you need to carry over to work on tomorrow?

____

What did you learn about your business (or yourself) today that will serve you in the future?

____

Day 5: The Most Important Question

From a Six-Figure Sales Salary to Home Organization

Melisa Celikel is the owner and CEO of Make SHT Happen LLC. She's an NLP Certified Organizational Business Consultant who helps her clients organize their lives and businesses. Melisa is a first-generation American. Her father and brother were born in Turkey, and most of her family still lives there. She was born and raised in Southern California, where she graduated with a BA in sociology. Melisa soon landed a corporate human resources job, which ultimately led her to recruiting for biopharma companies.

Melisa also consulted for Fortune 100, 200, and 500 companies. Even though she was earning a decent living, Melisa was burned out. She wanted to start her own company. Before deciding what kind of company that would be, Melisa completed the same exercise you did on Day 1. She inventoried her skills, experience, knowledge, financial situation, and network. Melisa was always neat, tidy, and clean as a child. *Very* clean. A psychiatrist once diagnosed her with obsessive-compulsive disorder (OCD).

For Melisa, a business based on organizing just made sense. She monetizes her natural gifts as a tidy, minimalistic person and uses those to help others declutter and organize their lives. She considers herself part of the Marie Kondo movement—sparking joy, decluttering homes, and living a life of minimalism. Melisa's business evolved from services to products. Now she offers online courses and B2B office organization consulting.

Before Melisa started her home organization business, she had to answer the most important question: **Is this business idea viable?** So, how did Melisa find her answer? How did she identify her potential customers and their buying habits, assess her competition, and come up with a price range for her services?

Assess the Market Viability of Your Offering

Market viability is essentially these three things: **market size, competition**, and **profitability**.

Market viability can be overwhelming. I've spent hours and even days analyzing market viability in the past. So, what's my suggested approach based on Melisa's experience, my own personal experience, and the countless entrepreneurs I've interviewed? Here's what I've realized. There is no perfect way to identify your market viability. Your initial answers will continue to evolve the more you learn.

For now, your goal is to complete just enough research to have some basic information on your future customers, a list of your top competitors, and a price range for your offering so you can start your business. With that in mind, pick two offer ideas from Day 3 that you want to check for viability. Not just one. Pick two ideas and spend today answering the following questions about them:

1. **Market Size:** Are there (enough) paying customers for your product? What customers will buy this offering?
2. **Competition:** How many competitors do you have? How strong are those competitors?
3. **Profitability:** Can you make a profit selling your offering? What is the potential price range for you to be profitable as well as getting a stream of paying customers?

Let's research your customers' overall interest in your industry by using freely available tools like **Google Keyword Planner**. Google Keyword Planner is an outstanding free tool that tells you the average monthly search volume for your specific query and a general idea of your competition. Depending on your offering, you can look at the reviews on platforms such as Yelp to get an idea of how many competitors you have and their quality of service.

I highly recommend you also visit your top competitors' websites and sign up for any mailing lists to get an idea of their offerings and prices. In Melisa's hometown in San Diego County, there are over two hundred professional home organizers. She identified her top five competitors, scoped out their email marketing strategies, signed up for their email lists, and followed them on social media. She even called a few as a ghost client to find out their pricing. Based on her research, Melisa started out charging $200 per four-hour session and later increased that to $300.

Market Viability: Now It's Your Turn

Check off the box beside each task as you complete it. Use the following example of Melisa's business and fill in your own information as you go along.

Service offered: Professional Organizing

Category	List, Description	Notes
Overall trends and observations	Medium to high interest throughout the year; peak demand in January (Using Google Trends)	
Search volume of keywords:	10K to 100K per month (for professional organizer) ~10K per month (home organization)	
Target customers	Women; Age range 30 to 50 years	
Competition	Competition: Medium	
	Competitor 1	website
	Competitor 2	website
	Competitor 3	website
Product price range	Overall range $75 per hour to $150 per hour (Minimum of 2 hours to 4 hours purchase)	
	Sweet spot: $100 per hour (for 2 hours minimum)	

❑ **1. Use Google Trends to determine overall customer interest: 5 minutes**

Go to Google Trends and enter your market offering (example: home organization, professional organizer). This will tell you overall interest, trends over time, and seasonality. Note any useful information in your spreadsheet.

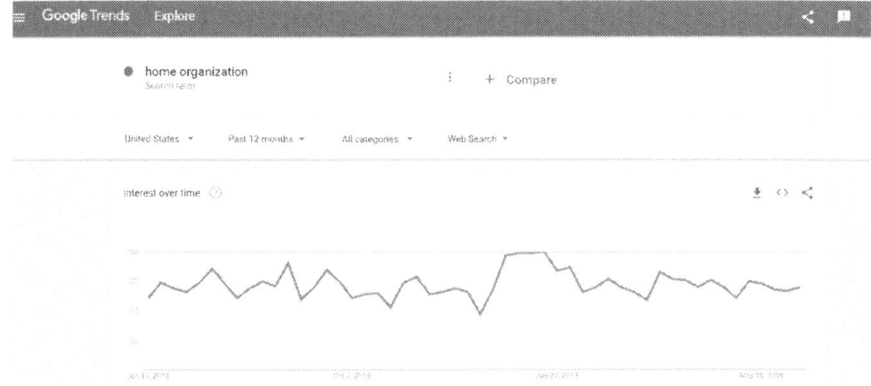

Google Trends will also show you additional information, such as high-interest geographies, related topics, and queries.

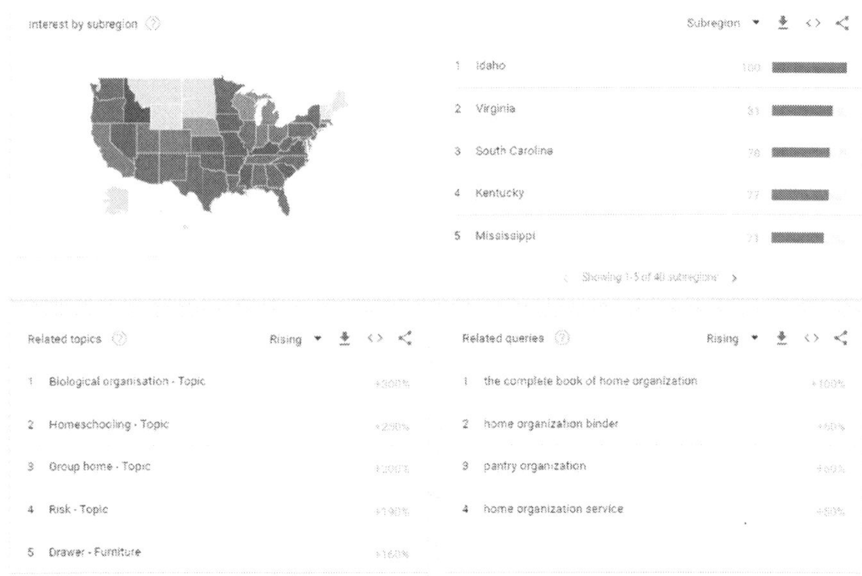

- ❑ **2. Complete a Google Keyword Planner analysis: 15 minutes**

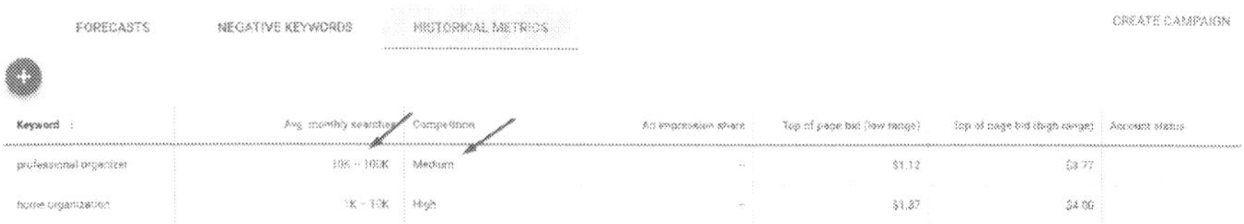

FORECASTS NEGATIVE KEYWORDS HISTORICAL METRICS CREATE CAMPAIGN

Keyword	Avg. monthly searches	Competition	Ad impression share	Top of page bid (low range)	Top of page bid (high range)	Account status
professional organizer	10K – 100K	Medium	–	$1.12	$3.77	
home organization	1K – 10K	High	–	$1.37	$4.00	

- ❑ **3. Research key competitors in your area, their offerings, and their pricing: 20 minutes**

  Yelp and Craigslist can be a great tool for researching competitors for local services like professional organizer or home organization.

- ❑ **4. Explore your industry's forums: 20 minutes**

  Search for specific forums in your industry. On Google, search for the following: "your industry forum" (example: home organization forum or professional organizer forum). Spend a few minutes on a few forums to get an idea of what price range your competitors are charging and what their offerings are.

Daily Standup

Did you complete today's tasks?

- ❑ Yes
- ❑ No

If no, what do you need to carry over to work on tomorrow?

What did you learn about your business (or yourself) today that will serve you in the future?

Day 6: The Price May Be Right

To Sell a Fish or Teach People to Catch One?

Janet Elie didn't love her career. She'd spent over thirty years in the financial services industry in marketing and management. Nearing retirement, Janet wanted to do something with more impact. After hearing Tony Robbins speak, she decided to start a business helping insurance agents find better customers. And ... nothing. No matter what she tried, she couldn't get insurance agents to become her paying customers.

That's when she changed course. She paired up with her sister, Gillian Whitney, and together they started

Launch4Life.com. The sisters decided to train tech-savvy small business owners to do their own SEO for a fraction of the cost of paying an SEO agency. Janet had coached and trained small business owners on how to adapt to the social media world. Gillian had over twenty years of experience in the communications and training industry and already had the skills and experience needed to teach, coach, and mentor clients. As soon as they found the right customers, the business took off. Janet and Gillian quickly learned that pricing is important to landing customers and that it almost always takes some trial and error before you get it right.

Different Business Models Require Different Pricing Strategies

Pricing is an important piece of the puzzle, and you probably won't get it right on your first try. I don't mean to sound like a downer, but any successful entrepreneur will tell you—correct pricing takes experimentation. The important thing is to use guidelines to get you as close to the mark as possible.

Janet and Gillian didn't get it right the first time. They iterated and eventually settled on something that felt right for them and their customers. Instead of doing SEO for their ideal clients, they found they could teach them how to do it themselves, significantly lowering their price point. This was their sweet spot. To find your own sweet spot, you first need to decide if you'll charge hourly prices or flat rates (or some combination of the two). Here's a chart to help you:

	Pros	Cons	When to Use
Hourly Price	Popular, easily understood, earn for what you work	Caps earnings, punishes efficiency	New to freelancing, ad hoc work, unfamiliar/unstructured jobs
Fixed Price	Simple, budget-friendly, maximize earnings	Risk underselling, inflexible, hard sell	Well-scoped work, short projects, budget-conscious clients, trusted relationships

Beyond that, there are five basic pricing strategies you can use. Here are their basics:

	What It Is	When To Use
Cost-plus pricing	Calculate all your costs and add your profit margin	Typically used for products when you can identify all costs
Competitive pricing	Set a price based on what your competition is charging	Use it if you know your competition and have a general idea of their prices
Value-based pricing	Price based on what the customer perceives is the value of your offering	Somewhat difficult to figure out; use it if you have a unique offering
Price skimming	Start with premium price and reduce over time	Use it if you are the first in your category
Penetration pricing	Set a lower price to get a foothold and increase over time	Use it when you are new and don't have many referrals

Today's task is figuring out which pricing strategy you'll use and the number amount you'll start with. Yes, you can still get clients with imperfect pricing. Don't worry. You're still on track to have a paying client by day thirty.

Decide on Your First Pricing Strategy and Price Point

Check off the box beside each task as you complete it.

- ❑ **1. Review your competition and their prices: 20 minutes**

  To get an idea of what your target market is used to, look up your competition's pricing. Do they charge hourly? Sell packaged deals? Do they price competitively? Or do their prices vary greatly for the same services?

- ❑ **2. Choose the pricing strategy that makes sense to you: 30 minutes**

  Are you offering a service or a product? What are your upfront costs to deliver your product or service? How much of a profit margin do you need to make? Do you want to get as many customers as possible, or do you want to be a premium leader in the market? Take some time to write down your answers and compare them with the pricing strategies in this chapter. Which one makes the most sense to start with?

- ❑ **3. Decide your price and write down the justification: 10 minutes**

  Now that you know your pricing strategy, choose a price to start with. Remember, don't expect to stick to this price forever. It's a starting point. For today, write down the price point you'll start at and your reasons behind it. This way, when you do adjust your pricing, you can do it systematically and based on logic.

Daily Standup

Did you complete today's tasks?

❑ Yes

❑ No

If no, what do you need to carry over to work on tomorrow?

____

What did you learn about your business (or yourself) today that will serve you in the future?

____

Day 7: Setting up Your Business

Accounting for Passive Income

Alina Trigub is the founder and managing partner of SAMO Financial, a boutique private equity firm that specializes in wealth preservation and tax strategies, including passive real estate investing. Alina empowers her clients to take control of their financial future and build a legacy for themselves and generations to come while positively impacting communities where they invest. Alina ensures that her clients learn how to invest in real estate with minimal involvement, only pursuing investments that work best for their unique situation, expectations, and goals. Each investment is completely passive so that clients can concentrate on their everyday lives, families, careers, and businesses.

Why do people need a service like Alina's? Why not just buy property, find tenants, and collect rent yourself? Imagine you purchase a rental property. It's your first real investment. You're excited about becoming a landlord. Since you've closed on the house, you can sit back, relax, and collect the rent. Right? Wrong. At 2:00 a.m., phone calls pour in from tenants. Pipes in the basement froze and started leaking. Your plumber just left for vacation. Guess who's going to bundle up (because it's 12 degrees outside) and drive to the property to try and fix the pipes? That's right. *You.*

Now imagine you worked with SAMO Financial. With Alina's guidance, you invest in an apartment building syndication. Dividends roll into your bank account every quarter. Apartments are gradually renovated to attract higher-paying tenants. After two or three years, the apartment building value has appreciated. When the building is reappraised, you receive a portion of your equity money back. Dividends continue to stream into your account. When the building is sold in five to ten years, you'll receive the final portion of the proceeds. In short, you get to watch your money grow while not having to be responsible for frozen pipes. Or any other issues that come along. That's what Alina's business model is all about.

Before starting her own business, Alina earned a bachelor's degree in accounting from Baruch College of the City University of New York and an MBA in finance and management from Rutgers University. She then worked as a tax accountant at Ernst & Young and later for some other private companies. How in the world did she end up in real estate? Well, for years Alina wanted to lower the tax burden for her family by applying the principles she learned as a tax accountant. For years, she was interested in real estate but hadn't taken action. Finally, she took action and started researching real estate investing, learned about passive investments via syndications, and began investing. Diversifying her portfolio worked out so well, she figured why not help other investors do the same?

SAMO Financial was born. In the past few years, Alina has helped clients acquire and invest in over 1,200 apartment units, a $10 million self-storage fund, and an over $5 million mobile home parks fund. When Alina talks to potential investors, she's eager to hear about their goals. Together, they explore ways to improve portfolios, such as moving capital from volatile Wall Street investments into safer real estate assets.

Investing in a Good Name

So, how did Alina come up with the name SAMO Financial? First of all, she didn't spend time stressing out over what she'd call her business. And she didn't have to go too far in coming up with one. She simply took the first name initials from her family members—S, A, M, O—and voilà! Business name, check. There is no "right" way to come up with a business name.

Next, Alina had to decide on a legal structure. Unfortunately, entrepreneurship in the digital age isn't like selling lemonade in your front yard as a kid. You have to complete and submit paperwork to the government so that the authorities know your business exists. (Don't worry, we'll cover that—and it won't take hours and hours!)

Like Alina, you get to decide among a sole proprietorship, partnership, corporation, and limited liability company (LLC). Given that Alina's business involves extensive legal work, she needed a capable attorney who specialized in real estate. She researched real estate attorneys online, asked colleagues for referrals, and picked an attorney to help structure and support her business as she grew. Alina, her attorney, and her accountant (yes, accountants need accountants, too!) got together in one room and went through the pros and cons of possible legal structures for her business. With their guidance, she decided on an LLC. For entrepreneurs who care about getting revenue as fast as possible (and keeping as much as possible), LLCs make the most sense. You'll soon learn why.

Business Name and Legal Structure: Now It's Your Turn

Check off the box beside each task as you complete it.

❑ **1. Select a business name: 10 minutes**

Naming your business can feel like naming a child. It's not that important, but it sure feels that way. Over the years, I've met entrepreneurs who spent tens of thousands of dollars on branding consultants to come up with the perfect business name. Don't waste your money or your time. Why are you starting this business? To get customers. That's your single objective. So your goal for your business name should be selecting one that doesn't *repel* potential customers. That's it. My best advice is to pick whatever comes to mind when you think about the people you want to help and what you want to offer. It can be anything. This isn't a science.

Got a business name in your head? Great. Now, to make sure your name won't push customers away, follow these simple rules:

- Search your business name online to confirm it's not already taken.
- Avoid hard-to-spell names (e.g., Acquaintance Inc.).
- Don't pick a name that limits your business as you grow (e.g., Only Pine Candles LLC).
- Use a name that gives people a clue what you do (e.g., Internet Marketers of Indiana).
- Keep it simple and short (e.g., Purely Sweet Baked Goods).
- Don't copycat other businesses (e.g., The North Face Book Printing Company).
- Stay away from random or annoying words (e.g., Bleeding Hounds Popcorn).
- Don't use industry jargon people don't know (e.g., Onomatopoeia Freelance Editing).

Does your business name idea pass the test? If not, run your next idea through the rules until it passes. If so, congratulations! You're ready to move on to step two.

❑ **2. Secure your domain name: 10 minutes**

You have a business name, and you know the matching domain name isn't taken (e.g., www.YourBusinessName.com). Now it's time to go buy it! Take ten minutes and go to www.GoDaddy.com right now to claim your name online. It should cost you no more than fifteen dollars. That's it. That's all you have to do.

❑ **3. Register your business with the government: 30 minutes**

If your business isn't registered with the government, it's not a real business. If an angry customer takes legal action against your business for any reason, you are held personally liable. They could sue you, seize your bank accounts, and take your house. Unlikely, but possible. It's hard to serve your paying customers if one of them gets angry and has you thrown out onto the street. Better safe than sorry—make your business a legal entity. What do I mean by legal entity? Well, you've seen the types of business structures already:

- Sole proprietorship
- Partnership
- Corporation
- Limited liability company

If you're not pursuing outside investors, teaming up with other people, or planning to sell shares of ownership in your company, go with an LLC. When your business becomes a limited liability company, you and your business are now separate entities. Disgruntled customers can send their lawyer sharks after your business, but not after you and your family. Thank goodness!

What about taxes? Businesses pay taxes just like employees do. In the United States, the Internal Revenue Service (IRS) automatically classifies an LLC as either a partnership or a sole proprietorship. If you're the sole owner of your business, your LLC is a sole proprietorship. That's the case for 99 percent of the people reading this book.

All you need to file for an LLC is your business name and some cash. LLC state filing fees range between $50 and $500. The average filing fee for an LLC in the United States is $127. To download your LLC paperwork, file for an LLC, and pay the fee, go to www.The60MinuteStartup.com for the most up-to-date website links.

❑ **4. Find legal representation (should you need it): 10 minutes**

Filing the paperwork for your LLC is quick and easy, so you shouldn't need an attorney like Alina did. However, smart entrepreneurs always have a general business attorney and an intellectual property (IP) attorney in their contacts, should they need them. A general business attorney will be able to answer any questions that come up around customer contracts, agreements, or terms and conditions. An IP attorney will help you protect anything you create for your business from theft by competition. If you don't know any attorneys already, the fastest way to find trustworthy attorneys is to google "business attorney" and "IP attorney" followed by your country or state. Bookmark the business attorney and the IP attorney with the best reviews or add them to your contacts. You're all set for today.

Daily Standup

Did you complete today's tasks?

❑ Yes

❑ No

If no, what do you need to carry over to work on tomorrow?

____

What did you learn about your business (or yourself) today that will serve you in the future?

____

Day 8: Protect Your Success

The Lean (and Fit) Startup

Michelle Miller is a personal trainer and group exercise instructor in Tallahassee, Florida. For over twenty years, she's worked with people of all ages and fitness levels, but her passion is children's fitness. So how did this passion translate into her business?

As a young mother, Michelle's time with her first son went by fast. When she and her husband had their second son, she knew she wanted to be more present. Yes, she'd developed a special bond with her older son, but she wanted the same relationship with her younger son from the start.

One Sunday afternoon, Michelle was lying in bed with her five-year-old as he napped. Her twenty-year-old son sat on the floor reading while her husband's lawnmower buzzed rhythmically outside the window. Since she and her husband both worked full time, they didn't have a lot of family time together. So Michelle soaked up every minute with her kids she could. As she stared up at the glow stars on the ceiling, her mind wandered. She thought about what a happy child her youngest was. How connected she felt to him. How proud she was. Even as young children, both Michelle's sons stayed in good shape. They kept up with all the adults whenever they hiked or swam as a family with friends.

Michelle then thought about other families and their children. *How do those other parents connect with their kids? I'm a fitness trainer, and I'm great at what I do. I know how to help my kids be healthy and strong. Physical activity has given us something we can connect over,* she thought. *What do other people have if they're great at their jobs? A great doctor, lawyer, or English teacher? How do they bond with their kids? How do they help their kids get active and healthy? Do they buy a family exercise program?*

Michelle got out of bed and googled around. She went on Amazon, Walmart, and other online stores. She was shocked—she found no quality physical training for children.

Everything labeled "kids' fitness" was fluff or ads for dumbed-down exercise equipment. *Free weights? No. No, that's a playset. Pretend exercise is not exercise.* Then and there, Michelle made it her mission to change family fitness forever.

I'm going to create a step-by-step fitness program that will teach anybody. You can have zero skills and still follow my program. You can be fit but not know how to be active with your kids. I'm going to make it so easy for kids to work out that they can exercise together with their parents.

And so www.MyFirstWorkout.com (MM Fitness LLC) was born. From March 2018 through the fall, Michelle developed her logo, branding, and custom exercise equipment for her future clients. She wanted her exercise-at-home kit to include equipment like weights, jump rope, and an exercise mat as well as programming suitable for parents and children. When she learned she couldn't buy dumbbells in large quantities in the United States for a reasonable price, she partnered with vendors in China.

For her program, Michelle designed twelve different exercise posters with pictures and detailed instructions on how to perform each exercise. She recorded twelve different videos with 123 different exercises, which corresponded to her posters. Even as Michelle worked on her business, she kept the project hidden. Only when the whole kit was ready was it time to show the world the fruits of her labor. Michelle scheduled a big launch at the Las Vegas ABC Expo in October 2018.

"Wow!" One woman's eyes lit up as she studied the posters at Michelle's booth. "This is... I've never seen anything like this. Kids need this. So do parents! How do I find out more?"

From there, Michelle joined Amazon and was featured on Zulily and *ABC News*. She got her program featured in magazines. By December 2018, Michelle's first product was released, and it hit Jacksonville in time for the Christmas holiday.

Michelle's business isn't just about physical fitness. It's also about connecting children with their parents or any caregiver in their life. Fitness affects your health, how you care for and feel about your body, your relationships, how you do in school, and even your career success later in life. Improving quality of life for families everywhere is what My First Workout is all about.

Getting Your Business in Shape

Before Michelle launched MM Fitness LLC, she had to register her business with federal and state government agencies, pass inspections, get business licenses, and purchase insurance. After all, Michelle was importing goods manufactured in China, and young children used her products. If any business needed a federal business license and product liability insurance, it was Michelle's! She had no reason to expect her program or fitness products were defective, but better to plan for the worst-case scenario than to have it surprise you out of business.

For every business I've started, I have always gone through the same checklist. Early on, my checklist didn't include licenses and insurance. Then I found out about them... the hard way. One of my clients asked me for proof of my licenses and general liability insurance, and I had neither. Don't worry—I'll make sure you're not scrambling to get them like I was!

Tax IDs, Licenses, Insurance: Now It's Your Turn

Check off the box beside each task as you complete it.

- ❑ **1. Apply for government tax IDs: 20 minutes**

  First, let's start with the easy stuff—tax IDs. Every business needs a federal tax ID (also called an "EIN") as well as a state tax ID. The federal tax ID/EIN is what you'll need to open a bank account, file tax returns, and apply for your business license (step two).

  Go to the IRS' website and fill out the Federal Tax ID Application. During the tax ID application process, the IRS asks you to provide basic information including your business structure (e.g., LLC), the type of organization you operate (e.g., consulting), and your name and address. When you get to the field that asks for the "responsible party," put your name there. Unless you have a business partnership, you alone are responsible for your tax ID application. The responsible party needs to have a valid taxpayer identification number (e.g., social security number) to apply.

After you submit your federal tax ID application, go to your state's secretary of state website (i.e., google "Iowa secretary of state website") and apply for a state tax ID. The state forms are similar to the federal ones. For the most up-to-date IRS and state tax ID application forms, go to www.The60MinuteStartup.com.

- [ ] **2. Apply for business licenses: 20 minutes**

According to the United States Small Business Administration, most small businesses need a combination of licenses and permits from both federal and state agencies. The requirements—and fees—vary based on your business activities, location, and government rules. For example, if your business broadcasts information by radio, television, wire, satellite, or cable, you will need a license and permit to operate your business from the Federal Communications Commission. Or if you wholesale, import, or sell alcoholic beverages (e.g., gin-of-the-month subscription box), you may need both licenses and permits from the Alcohol and Tobacco Tax and Trade Bureau and the local alcohol beverage control board.

So how do you know what licenses your business needs? The SBA website tells you which federal or state license to apply for based on your industry and your state. Go to www.The60MinuteStartup.com for the most up-to-date SBA website links.

If your product or company is unique and doesn't fit into any of the listed industries, or if you're still unsure what licenses you need, pull out the business attorney's phone number that you bookmarked in the last chapter and call for a quick consult.

- [ ] **3. Apply for business insurance: 20 minutes**

You have car insurance. You have homeowner's or renter's insurance. You may even have life insurance. Why? To protect what you care about. The *people* you care about. Not just the stuff. Why are you building a sixty-minute startup? So you can take better care of yourself, your family, and your future. Just as you protect your property in case of damage or theft, you'll want to safeguard this important asset you're now building.

Just like there are different types of car insurance (e.g., liability, collision, comprehensive, etc.), there are different types of business insurance. You may not need all of them, so it's good to know your options before you get your first paying customers. Here are the different types of insurance you can purchase for your business:

- Business interruption insurance—covers loss of income after a disaster forces you to halt operations.
- Data breach insurance—covers damage, theft, or destruction of electronic records such as customers' personal information.

- General liability—covers several claims such as personal injury or property damage that happen during day-to-day business operations.
- Home-based business insurance—protects entrepreneurs working out of a home office from liability, property damage, and other claims. **Excellent choice for *The 60-Minute Startup* readers!**
- Product liability—covers claims related to product defects that hurt someone or damage property.
- Professional liability—protects service providers like consultants and freelancers from the legal fees arising from a customer's negligence claim, as well as any damages awarded in such a lawsuit.
- Property insurance—covers the repair or replacement costs of the space you use to operate your business, as well as everything inside and outside it, whether you own, rent, or live there.
- Vehicle insurance—covers accident damage and personal injury costs that happen while you or an employee is driving a company vehicle on business (e.g., a car accident on the way to meet a prospect for coffee).
- Workers' compensation—covers work-related accidents, sickness, and even death.

You have questions right now, don't you? *Do I just call one company and purchase all the plans from them? Do I have to apply for each one I want separately? Or do I ask my lawyer for help?* You'll be able to tell which kinds of insurance you'll need (and which ones you won't) just by looking at what kind of business you're starting. If you're not sure about some of them, call your business attorney again.

Daily Standup

Did you complete today's tasks?

❑ Yes

❑ No

If no, what do you need to carry over to work on tomorrow?

____

What did you learn about your business (or yourself) today that will serve you in the future?

____

Day 9: Set Up Shop Online

Zero to 70 Million Visitors—It Starts with a Simple Website

Jeff Rizzo has reached over 70 million people online. He's the founder and CEO of RIZKNOWS, the umbrella company for RizKnows.com, MySlumberYard.com, and other websites that get over four million views per month. Jeff has racked up over 100 million views on YouTube. Jeff is so good at what he does, RIZKNOWS is now backed by Haney Business Ventures, an early-stage investment firm in Sacramento, California.

Before all that, Jeff was a UC Berkeley graduate. He worked as a middle-marketing investment banker at Duff & Phelps, a good job according to anyone on the outside. Jeff got to help people raise capital, restructure balance sheets, and sell their businesses. He always had the desire to start his own business, though, so he started simple—with a website.

In Jeff's early entrepreneurial days, nothing separated him from any other entrepreneur. He was a guy who needed a website so he could run his own business. So he bought a domain name, built a website, and published educational content. Jeff realized he couldn't afford a sophisticated e-commerce site, so he pivoted. Jeff launched a new website, one that published unbiased product reviews rather than selling products. He spotted the trend that people watched more and more videos online, so he decided to ride that wave to the business success he enjoys today.

To come up with video content, Jeff and his team find popular products. They test them out and make interesting and entertaining videos of their reviews, all in a very anti-TV way. What you see on TV is polished. Professional. What Jeff likes to do is produce video content as though your neighbor gave you information. Authenticity is valuable.

Jeff and his team don't get paid to say good or bad things about a product; they just present exactly what they think. They choose products based on what the audience asks for as well as internet trends. They cover everything from technology to home goods, bedding, sports equipment, and outdoor gear. Jeff knows the vast majority of the audience are men in their midthirties, so all content caters to them as if Jeff is speaking peer to peer. This strategy keeps video views high and ensures previous visitors come back for more.

RIZKNOWS has a lot of competition. It's every media site out there. Everyone from *The Wall Street Journal* to *The New York Times* publishes reviews, he says. Every RIZKNOWS video has to be more informative and engaging than anyone else's product review. From the results, it looks like Jeff is doing a great job. RIZKNOWS is hugely successful, but it all started with a single website, which is our focus today. In my own businesses, I've owned over a thousand domains in the past fifteen years and have built websites in the double digits.

In 2016, I wanted to start a consulting business in the area of data analytics and digital transformation. I went through my business startup checklist and settled on three possible business names:

1. Digital Transformation Pro
2. Data Analytics Pro
3. DigTran Consultants

With those names, I went to GoDaddy.com to check availability. The second one was already taken, so I went with the first one (Digital Transformation Pro) and registered that domain name. If I wanted the second name anyway, I could've added something like "Inc." to the end of it, but I didn't want to limit myself to data analytics exclusively. With my domain name registered, it was time to set up the website. I could have outsourced the task, but I knew I could DIY it. I bought an easy-to-use WordPress theme and installed it on my website. I already had a web host for other websites, so I added the new domain name to my existing account. It took me about a day to get the basic website working with five pages.

With the website set up, I wanted to stay in touch with people who visited my site, so I used Mailchimp to set up my email marketing. I linked the email sign-up forms on my website with my Mailchimp account, and I was in business. You're about to be as well.

Your Key Web Assets: Domain Name, Website, Email Marketing

Domain Name

With the business name you picked out on Day 7, go to a domain name registrar (like GoDaddy, Namecheap, etc.) and do a domain name search. Going for a .com is usually the best rule of thumb, as this is the most popular and will likely bring you more visitors than a .net or a .org. If your business name is already taken, most name registrars will suggest other variations. Most of these are made by adding simple words to the beginning or end of your URL.

Website Design

This is where most people start sweating. They stress out over "designing a website," especially if it's something they've never done before. Don't stress out; just get something up and running. At this point, you don't need to worry about fancy design features. You just need a basic website that works. Most content management systems like WordPress or Shopify make setting up a basic site really easy. And, of course, it's something you can always outsource to an expert.

Email Marketing

It might sound a little boring, but I can't emphasize enough how important email marketing is. Chances are, it's where your first paying customer will come from. It doesn't matter which email marketing platform you choose, as long as you choose one. If you need a recommendation, I've used Mailchimp in the past and am happy with it. Once you create an account, create a couple of email sign-up forms on your website and link them to your email marketing platform. This way, you'll be able to market to people even after they leave your website.

Set Up Your Own Web Presence

Check off the box beside each task as you complete it.

- ❑ **1. Secure your domain name: 10 minutes**

  Go to your favorite domain registrar, and check for your business name plus .com. If it's available, buy it. If it's not available, use the registrar's recommendations to figure out another domain name and buy that one.

- ❑ **2. Set up and "design" your website: 25 minutes**

  Yes, you really can do this in less than half an hour. Most web hosts will offer a "one-step" install for WordPress. After you do that, you can install a ready-made theme and edit the content on the website to reflect your business. Don't overthink it. It'll be done before you know it.

I'd suggest spending today's twenty-five minutes making decisions about your website. Then either outsource to a web guy or take tomorrow to develop the website fully. Think about:

- Which content management system do you want to use? WordPress or something else?
- Which theme works best for you?
- What content do you want to have published when the website goes live?

My only advice no matter which route you choose is not to spend much time or money on your website right now. Our main focus is getting your first paying customers, and the fanciest website in the world won't guarantee that. Hard work in other areas will.

❑ **3. Email marketing integration: 25 minutes**

Every entrepreneur I've spoken to has said they wish they'd started email marketing sooner. Once your website is up and running, pick an email marketing platform like Mailchimp or AWeber and integrate it with your website. Here are some platforms you can choose from:

- Mailchimp
- AWeber
- Constant Contact

- SendinBlue
- ConvertKit

Daily Standup

Did you complete today's tasks?

❑ Yes

❑ No

If no, what do you need to carry over to work on tomorrow?

____

What did you learn about your business (or yourself) today that will serve you in the future?

____

Day 10: Money, Money, Money

The Dark Side of Accounting Led This Entrepreneur to the Light

Nicole Landau, Certified Fraud Examiner (CFE), started her career as an accountant for a large retailer who was in the midst of filing its initial public offering (IPO). Company changes shuffled her around and pushed her over to "the dark side," as she calls it, internal auditing. She then transitioned to a public accounting firm where she did "outsourced internal auditing" for banks, retail corporations, and IPO-bound companies. She made her final stop with a bank before launching as an entrepreneur. The bank went through a year-long merger, which caused the audits to be put on hold. Luckily for Nicole, this pause gave her time to question what she really wanted out of life.

Rather than being an auditor or accountant for one corporation, she wanted to use her skill set to help people who were in business for themselves. She wanted to be their trusted financial adviser. She didn't quit her job cold turkey and jump into a brand-new business immediately, though. She started her consulting business as a side hustle and eased into doing it full time. Her first client came from a referral within her network. That customer referred someone else, and her side hustle grew from there via referrals.

As more clients came in, she found herself wanting to help people in the construction industry, her first passion. She grew up around construction and even considered it as a career path. Early on in her career, Nicole wanted to be an architect, so she took classes to learn woodworking and CAD drawing. She and her husband even built two houses on their own. From her passion for construction and accounting, she founded Landau Consulting Solutions, which provides outsourced chief financial officer (CFO) services to construction businesses.

Most of Landau Consulting Solutions' clients are general contractors, so they may not have accountants on staff. Instead, they outsource their accounting to Landau. The firm handles accounts receivable, accounts payable, payroll, budgeting, and cash flow forecasting. They help contractors track their budget versus actuals and advise them on financial clarity in order to grow their businesses. As a result, her clients gain control over their finances, increase profits, and streamline their accounting. On top of that, Nicole's financial coaching helps them gain clarity on their current success level so they can see what needs to change to reach their next goal. The best part is that Landau Consulting Solutions serves clients all over the country. Today, they have monthly construction accounting clients from Virginia to California. On top of her monthly clients, she provides consulting, software implementation, and forensic accounting services. These services may include:

- Systems integration for clients who use different types of software. These businesses need software systems to "talk to each other" so that employees don't have to waste time on manual data entry.
- Consulting for brand-new contractor business owners who need help setting their finances up correctly so that they're profitable from month one.
- Cleaning up after clients who've tried and failed at doing their own accounting. Their records are a mess, and Nicole's team can clean them up.
- Forensic investigations for uncovering fraud.

After helping so many businesses, Nicole has settled her primary focus for all her consulting clients on financial clarity. It's critical to understand financial statements to make informed business decisions. Especially for construction businesses, cash flow is critical as subcontractors want their payments immediately, but revenue doesn't always come in at the same pace. In accounting terms, accounts receivable (money coming in) and accounts payable (money going out) must be monitored for the correct ratio. Getting the right financial systems in place is crucial for any business. It doesn't matter if you're running a side hustle or have a multimillion-dollar business. You need to know your numbers.

Get Your Bank Account, Accounting, and Payments Squared Away

A bank account, accounting software, and payment systems are must-haves when you're getting started. These three assets will keep your business and personal finances separate. This gives you a way to collect from your customers and pay your expenses. It also helps you track your cash flow so you can see the health of your business and identify areas where you can become more successful.

Open a Business Bank Account

I see two main reasons every entrepreneur needs a business bank account:

- To keep their personal and business finances separate.
- To have a clean record of their business revenue and expenses to make it easier to file taxes.

Nicole considers three factors when she helps a client open a bank account:

- The type of bank account: As a new business, go with a checking account instead of a savings account.

- Which bank to choose: This is a personal preference, but some things to consider include:
  - Banks you already use
  - Available ATMs
  - Online and mobile banking options
  - Integration with bookkeeping software
  - Available services like lines of credit, overdraft protection, loans, and credit cards
  - Long-term relationships in the event additional funding is needed
- The costs of an account: Some banks charge monthly fees depending on the balance carried.

When opening a bank account, you may be required to provide some or all of these documents:

Legal Structure	Personal or Business Identification	Organization Documents	Business Licenses
Sole Proprietorship	Personal identification (SSN etc.)	Fictitious business name (or DBA) (optional)	As needed for your business
Partnership	Federal Employer Identification Number (EIN)	Partnership agreement	As needed for your business
S Corp/C Corp	Federal Employer Identification Number (EIN)	Articles of incorporation Corporate charter/resolution	As needed for your business
Limited Liability Corporation	Federal Employer Identification Number (EIN)	Organizational forms as required for partnership or S Corp	As needed for your business

Choose an Accountant (Or Accounting Software)

Using accounting software, an accountant, or both depends on your business model and your personality. All I need is cloud-based accounting software. Some entrepreneurs just write transactions down on paper and send them to their accountant. Nicole, obviously, is an accountant herself. All she needed was bookkeeping software. So how do you choose accounting software or an accountant? Consider these four points:

- Does your sales setup need specialized software, like inventory or invoicing capabilities?
- Would you prefer to buy a software license outright and keep your records on your computer? Or would you prefer to pay month to month and keep your records in the cloud?
- If you choose a monthly payment plan, will you need add-ons? Like paying more to send more invoices or to accept online payments?
- Does your accountant have software preferences?

Some popular accounting software includes Freshbooks, Quickbooks, Wave, Xero, and Zoho Books. Nicole uses Freshbooks for invoicing and expense tracking and takes care of the rest herself. Use what the professionals use!

Decide How You'll Get Paid

Finally, decide how people will pay you. If your customers can't pay you, they can't become your customers, and your business can't make money. That should go without saying, but it often doesn't. PayPal is a popular way for online businesses to accept payment. Other payment processors include Square and Stripe. Don't waste time comparing pros and cons. These three solutions allow you to invoice customers for services and create product checkout pages, so pick one and move on to finding customers so you can get paid.

Set Up Your Money Systems

Check off the box beside each task as you complete it.

❑ **1. Prepare to open your bank account: 15 minutes**

Decide on the bank you'll use and the type of account you'll open. It will probably be a checking account. Organize any required paperwork to take into your bank. Here's one caveat—we talked about applying for your EIN two days ago, so you might not have it back yet. If that's the case, wait on this step.

❑ **2. Find your accountant (or accounting software): 30 minutes**

Look through the accounting software that is relevant to your niche and choose the one that works best for you. Create an account and link it to your new bank account. If you know an accountant through friends or family, reach out to them. Otherwise, don't waste half the day looking at online reviews for local CPAs. Go with the software instead.

- ❑ **3. Set up a payment system: 15 minutes**

  Pick a payment processing system and set up a new account. These accounts are free and only take a few minutes to set up. Connect your new account to your bank to make future money transfers easier.

Daily Standup

Did you complete today's tasks?

- ❑ Yes
- ❑ No

If no, what do you need to carry over to work on tomorrow?

____

What did you learn about your business (or yourself) today that will serve you in the future?

____

Day 11: Let's Talk Numbers

Build a Sales Pipeline Because You'll Always Have Money to Make

Kristie Jones has sales in her blood. Before starting her own business—Sales Acceleration Group—she ran sales development for a Silicon Valley company. She's an accidental entrepreneur. She developed a career with an extensive background in sales. With her promotion to director of a venture-backed firm called Gainsight, she thought she was set. Their headquarters sat in the middle of Silicon Valley and had about $150 million in funding. All good.

Until company changes disbanded Kristie's team. Kristie knew she'd be without a job soon. Being so good at what she did, she decided to move her team out from under the sales department and into marketing. The only catch was that the marketing team was located in Phoenix. Gainsight paid Kristie to stay on while they made the switch, but she started looking for a new job ASAP. After all, she still had a child at home to take care of.

Kristie reached out to people she thought might need a VP of Sales. She soon discovered people didn't want to hire her full time but *did* want her help as a consultant. She took consulting jobs that came along and soon realized that this season of transition was the perfect time to start her own company. Since college, Kristie had dreamed of one day owning her own business, but she never felt the nudge to go ahead and start one. The universe conspired around Kristie, so she followed her destiny into entrepreneurship.

But a few great clients in the beginning don't guarantee a solid business model. Sure, it was a great way to transition out of her old job, but was it something she could do forever? One thing Kristie knew was that to have a successful business, you have to have a healthy sales pipeline. Her first few clients came from companies she interviewed with in pursuit of a full-time job or from her earlier network. This was great, but these early, lucky opportunities didn't ensure a career's worth of new clients. To keep her business afloat, she always made sure her pipeline had at least three customers in it.

So Kristie went about building her pipeline. She noticed that more than 65 percent of her LinkedIn contacts were local. Face-to-face meetings are important to any type of consulting work, so she started cultivating these local relationships. This outreach helped Kristie fill up her sales pipeline for reliable clientele in the future. She also joined meet-ups, VC-backed events, and women's support groups as a way to flesh out her local network. She then volunteered for local charities as a way to further expand in the community.

With this dedication to creating a sales pipeline, Kristie built Sales Acceleration Group into the company it is today. Sales Acceleration Group specializes in helping small and midsize companies who are ready to scale and is basically a one-stop shop for all things growth. Her business also helps tech startups with sales strategy, processes, hiring, coaching, and training. She loves helping other entrepreneurs grow their revenue.

After her first few clients, Kristie also got better at pricing, which in turn helped her land more clients. She struggled delivering her services at an hourly rate, so she started pricing her services based on deliverables instead. As soon as a client agreed to the deliverables, it was easy to talk pricing. . . rather than the other way around.

All this said, the focus of this book is to help you get your first paying customers. But if you don't also build up a sales pipeline, your company will crash after you find your first few customers. Plus, if building a sales funnel is easy, that tells you that you've got a viable business idea. If it's hard, you know you might need to tweak your business plan a bit. Kristie also knew this, so she never stopped prospecting for new clients. She sent out newsletters, went to local meet-ups for entrepreneurs to grab drinks, and attended tech startup accelerator events. Filling your sales pipeline is crucial... especially when you need a sales forecast to offset startup expenses.

Sales Forecasts and Startup Expenses: Is Your Business Viable?

When Kristie started Sales Acceleration Group, she wanted to make sure the business would be viable for at least one year. She didn't want to use external funding, which meant she had to create a sales forecast. Comparing this forecast with her startup expenses showed her the break-even point and when she'd start to make a profit. To figure out your own business's numbers, consider these four factors:

Sales Forecast

This is a realistic estimate of what you'll be able to sell and for how much. Since Kristie offered coaching and training services, she decided to do a year-long forecast. She took into consideration each contract lasting three to six months and only managing three clients at a time.

Startup Expenses

These include government fees, insurance, website, advertising, outsourcing, legal fees, software, and utilities. Whatever your startup fees are, list each one with the cost amount.

Funding Sources and Amounts

According to the Small Business Administration, more than 60 percent of businesses are self-funded. This means money to get the thing up and running either comes out of the owner's pocket or from the business's first few (or several) sales. This funding can also include money from investors or bank loans.

Break-Even Analysis

Your break-even point is when revenue exceeds expenses, and you start making a profit. For most businesses, the break-even point is much shorter with a customer pipeline in place. For product-based businesses, the break-even point takes longer. (Customers don't pay until products are built or services are delivered.)

Run Your Own Numbers: Sales Forecast and Startup Expenses

Check off the box beside each task as you complete it.

❑ **1. Prepare your sales forecast: 20 minutes**

Download the sales forecast from www.The60MinuteStartup.com to help you with this.

Doing a one-year sales forecast is ideal, but six months is OK, too. Be realistic about how many people you'll have in your pipeline, what you'll charge, and how long it'll take to serve each client.

- ❑ **2. Add up startup expenses and funding Sources: 20 minutes**

  Download the startup expenses and funding sources template from www.The60MinuteStartup.com. Make sure all your expenses are added, including any payments to repay a business loan. Don't forget to pay yourself!

- ❑ **3. Do your break-even analysis: 20 minutes**

  If you use the template mentioned in the other two steps, this will already be done for you. Use these twenty minutes to look it over and make sure you're happy with it. If not, are there any adjustments you can make? If you've decided not to use the template, compare your startup expenses to how much money you'll make each month. How long will you work before you reach your break-even point?

Daily Standup

Did you complete today's tasks?

- ❑ Yes
- ❑ No

If no, what do you need to carry over to work on tomorrow?

____

What did you learn about your business (or yourself) today that will serve you in the future?

____

Day 12: An Agile Approach to Business Branding

Building a Strong Brand after a Shaky Start

Joellyn Sargent lived the life everyone said she should want. Career success. Marketing executive role. Happily married. But she still felt like something was missing.

After Joellyn and her husband lost their Florida home in a hurricane, they moved to a small town in Tennessee just a few weeks after their first child was born. Joellyn was only twenty-six, but she went with all the life changes and decided to start a business too. After a couple of strong years, Joellyn decided to shutter that business because of limited growth opportunities. She underestimated the power of personal connections in a small town, a blind spot that hindered her from establishing deep roots in the local market. She accepted a corporate marketing job with UPS and eventually moved on to more senior roles with other companies in the Atlanta area. Joellyn enjoyed her work, but the idea of entrepreneurship kept tugging at her. To satisfy her yearning, Joellyn started a side hustle selling fair-trade arts and crafts online.

Life went well until the stock market crashed, triggering the great recession. Joellyn knew her executive position in the mortgage industry wouldn't last, and she saw the down economy as an opportunity to start again. *If not now, when?*

Like any entrepreneur, Joellyn faced some challenges building her new business. She's an optimist at heart, and her naturally positive outlook helped her through the setbacks. When something went wrong , she didn't let herself wallow in it. She gave herself a day to be miserable or to do something fun and get some perspective. Then she went back at it. She was too passionate about what she did to let her dreams flop. Never discount determination.

Eventually, Joellyn sharpened her focus on helping other entrepreneurs, especially people who wanted to start a new business or those who had an established business but weren't satisfied with it. In short, Joellyn wanted to help out people in her shoes—people with the potential to be successful who needed some guidance to get there. Joellyn had a knack for helping companies who'd experienced massive growth that had slowed or stalled. They needed help figuring out why the slowdown happened and how to reverse it. Her skill set was a perfect match to help them figure it out and lead them back to success.

Joellyn decided to stick to her niche and only market to these ideal customers. Also trying to market to marketing executives within established companies wouldn't cut it. Developing close partnerships with her clients was important to her. Having clients who trusted her would let her help them in bigger ways. Together, they could burst through their fears, challenges, and marketing issues to achieve the growth they wanted.

Most importantly, Joellyn didn't try to build her new consulting business the way she grew her marketing agency. Instead, she leveraged her experience and built her brand through thought leadership. Joellyn blogged, contributed articles, and wrote books on marketing and branding including *Beyond the Launch*, *Is that You... Or Your Brand?* and *Meet Your Ideal Customer*. She gave talks on marketing and branding at conferences across the United States. Her generosity in sharing her expertise helped build trust and credibility with her audience, serving as a catalyst for growth in her business. Joellyn's reputation and visibility acted like a megaphone, delivering her message to her target audience loud and clear.

Along with these key brand builders, Joellyn used the powerful network she'd built over the years. Together with her brand, this network of entrepreneur contacts got Joellyn's consulting business off the ground. In fact, her first-ever customer came from a referral. When this sale happened, she knew her brand was effective—a total stranger trusted her enough to hire her. Her branding efforts had finally paid off.

The Key Brand Elements to Land Your First Paying Customers

Given that the main focus of this book is to get paying customers, branding may not seem important. Don't worry—I'm not going to tell you to write books and start doing public speaking like Joellyn did. Branding is important, though, so we'll come up with version one of your brand today. To me, a brand is a promise you deliver to your customers. Your brand tells people what they can expect from you and why they should buy from you. That's why we're using today's hour to focus on branding. It's essential to getting your first customers.

On Days 3 and 4, we figured out your offer and how to differentiate yourself from your competitors (also known as your unique value proposition, or UVP.) Today, we'll use that information to design visual brand elements to communicate what you offer. Joellyn took things to the next level and communicated her UVP consistently via books and speaking gigs. Before she could do that, her basic elements had to be in place. That's what we're focusing on today.

Brand Colors

According to color theory, brand colors can evoke strong emotional reactions. For example, light blue can help convey trust. Red can convey passion. Brown shows an earthy feel. Since you'll use your brand colors online and in your logo, pick out colors that make sense for what you offer. Don't overcomplicate it—just go with what looks right to your eyes.

Logo

Logos are the first thing most people will notice about your brand. You can spend hundreds of dollars on yours, or you can create one for free by making a plain-text logo. I've done both. I currently use a free plain-text logo for www.RameshDontha.com. Whether you outsource the design or do it yourself, the important thing is not to spend much time on it. Make sure your logo conveys the general meaning of your business and doesn't look bad. That's all you need. Good enough and done beats a beautiful work in progress.

Tagline

A tagline is a short, catchy way to summarize your unique value proposition. Use your UVP from your Day 4 homework and come up with a short, catchy statement. Here are some examples:

- Nike: Just Do It
- Sprite: Obey Your Thirst
- BMW: The Ultimate Driving Experience
- Ramesh Dontha: Build a Business, Start Today

Miscellaneous

Beyond your colors and your logo, you may want other branded items to help people remember you. These include business cards, social media headers, and other graphics used to advertise. These miscellaneous brand assets are optional, not essential. Create them only if you have extra time today. If not, don't worry. You won't lose customers if you don't have a business-branded header image above your social media profiles.

Create Your Own Branding in One Hour

Check off the box beside each task as you complete it.

❑ **1. Define your brand identity elements: 10 minutes**

Beyond a color palette and a logo, what other brand identity elements will you use? Business cards? Social media headers? Advertising images? Take a minute or two to jot down a list. After that, choose the colors you'll use as your brand's color palette.

❑ **2. Decide on a logo: 30 minutes**

First, decide if your logo is something you want to outsource or if you want to create it yourself. If you choose to do it yourself, use these thirty minutes to create a basic logo that integrates your brand colors. If you decide to outsource, use these thirty minutes to write a brief of what you want it to look like to send to a designer.

- ❑ **3. Write your tagline: 20 minutes**

  Starting with the UVP you came up with on Day 4, write a short, catchy tagline for your brand name.

- ❑ **4. Create your miscellaneous brand elements (optional): 10 Minutes**

  Will business cards play a part in your branding? What about social media header images? If so, use these ten minutes to design these assets. Incorporate your logo, tagline, and contact information. You can speed this process up by using the premade business card layouts at www.Canva.com.

Daily Standup

Did you complete today's tasks?

- ❑ Yes
- ❑ No

If no, what do you need to carry over to work on tomorrow?

____

What did you learn about your business (or yourself) today that will serve you in the future?

____

Day 13: The Dreaded Business Plan That Isn't That Hard

Evolving Eight Times in Five Years

When Phil Strazzulla finished Harvard Business School in 2014, he decided to start his own company right away. He'd done his college internship at a company of one and was floored by how much impact a one-person company could make. Phil felt like his experience, knowledge, and skill set could be valuable to the world, so he founded a human resources software company that was then called LifeGuides to help companies market themselves as a place to work. At the start, the business did well. He landed some marquee customers, but when the time came for those customers to renew their subscriptions, they didn't. When Phil called his customers to find out why, they admitted they'd bought his software and never used it. So when renewal time came, why keep paying?

Phil's business plan had an obvious problem, so he tweaked it again and again. He stayed revenue focused in order to pay the bills and worked closely with customers to build an iteration of the original product that would be valuable to his customers. By staying lean in his personal and professional life, Phil survived true startup mode for several years. The product had always looked good in sales presentations. Now, it also delivered value to the end user. The retention rate is now over 95 percent.

Today, Phil's entrepreneurial pursuits in the human resources space look a lot different from the original LifeGuides. Phil is now owner of Select Software Reviews, a website that offers unbiased reviews of human resources software tools. The website keeps both human resources and information technology professionals from wasting their time when searching for the right tools. In this new business, Phil doesn't make money selling his own software. Instead, he brings in revenue from software companies advertising on Select Software Reviews.

How did Phil finally find the right product-market fit? Well, Phil knew HR and IT managers had a problem finding the right tools for their companies. If or when they did find the right one, they ran into a lot of confusing advice on how to use it—or they never did. With Select Software Reviews, Phil helps managers cut through the clutter and make good, fast decisions based on their unique needs. One company might need to start using a customer relationship management system (CRM) for the first time while another business might need to upgrade to more robust payroll software that requires less manual work to keep records updated. Phil's free online guides take these specific needs into consideration. No more vague, confusing, or unhelpful advice about HR software. Just the exact solution for your business at your budget.

Phil learned something while going through his eight business iterations—customers don't change their behavior because an entrepreneur wants them to. Better to start a business that fits existing customer behaviors. It's a lot easier to do something that's already happening but in a better, faster, or cheaper way. For example, Uber makes getting a taxi ride a better, faster, and cheaper experience.

At first, Phil didn't realize that his software product would disrupt how his clients do things. But when they weren't implementing his software, it became obvious. He kept iterating his business plan—the agile way—and it paid off. Every entrepreneur can learn from Phil's success.

Your First Business Plan: Make It Quick and Dirty

It's pretty typical for a business to go through several business plan iterations in the early days. Phil started his business with a good plan, but he still needed to change it eight times before he found his sweet spot. I don't say this to discourage you from starting but to help you *just start.*

Unless you want to secure outside funding, you don't need a twenty-page business plan that'll take six days to write. All you need are the most essential elements to guide you. Nothing else. Your agile business plan won't take you more than an hour, and it'll fit onto a two-page document. Here are the key elements you need:

- Executive Summary
- Company Overview
- Business Description
- Market Analysis
- Operating Plan
- Marketing and Sales Plan
- Financial Plan

I'll describe each of these, but make sure you download the two-page business plan template at www.The60MinuteStartup.com.

Executive Summary

This comes first in business plan documents, but you write it last. It's an overview of your business, the problems you solve, your ideal customer, and your financial projections. Think of the Executive Summary as a high-level description of the company before you dive into the more detailed sections.

Company Overview

This includes your company summary, your products and services, and your mission statement. It also talks about how you got started, your position in the market, how you'll operate, and your financial goals. It's a short, succinct section that tells the reader what your business will do and how it's organized.

Business Description

This describes your company in terms of market need, your unique solution, and your value proposition. It addresses the opportunity you have with the problem you're solving and market demand for it. Then you discuss your offer in more detail, along with your pricing structure. You'll also talk about your value proposition, market need, and solution in detail. Here's what to include:

- **Value Proposition:** If you had to sum up the value you provide to your customers, what would you say? What makes you unique? Imagine you're playing by Twitter's old rules and only have 140 characters to sum it up. Keep it to one sentence.
- **Market Need:** What problems do your customers have? How do you reduce them? If you don't know the answer to this, it'll be hard to build a business. If you don't have answers to these questions yet, talk to your potential customers. Find out what they like about your product

or service. Why would they choose you over someone else?

- **Your Solution:** If someone asked you what you sell, what would your answer be? Your solution is the product or service you offer to solve the customer's problem. Describe this solution and why it's better than the alternatives.

Market Analysis

This shows how well you understand the needs of your market. It goes into the specifics of your industry and your ideal customer. You'll list things like age, gender, habits, geographic location, and buyer characteristics. You'll discuss the needs the market has and how those needs are being met by you and your competitors.

Sometimes business owners like to do a SWOT analysis in this section. SWOT stands for strengths, weaknesses, opportunities, and threats. This analysis helps them improve their market positioning even more.

If you have direct competitors, do your research and list your discoveries here. What products and services do your customers buy instead of yours? How is your business different from the competition? What makes your offer better than what's already out there?

Operating Plan

This section of your business plan tells how your company is organized and how you plan to develop as your company grows. It's a guide to how your business works.

Who has what management responsibilities? What dates and budgets will you meet to track results? What future growth goals do you want to meet?

You'll talk about how your business will launch your product or service to the market and how you'll support your customers. This section isn't theory—it's the logistics, technology, and grunt work involved in making your new business happen.

If you're launching a business with more than one person, you'll talk about your team in the Operating Plan section. Why did you choose certain people for certain job roles? If it's only you, write a few bullet points about why you're the right person to start and run this specific business.

Finally, if you're using partners or other resources to help your business grow, list them. Tell why they're important to your success.

Marketing and Sales Plan

Marketing and sales are two of the most important functions in any business. How will you promote your business to get sales? How will you get people into the sales pipeline you planned on Day 11? This is what you talk about in this section. Describe your key marketing messages and the channels you'll use to bring in leads for new customers. If you plan to buy ads, talk about your ad-buying strategy. Also list your sales channels. What are the places (online or offline) where you'll sell your products? Expect this section to take shape over the next two weeks or so.

Financial Plan

This is the last section of your business plan. It's time to assign numbers to ideas. Here you list your estimated sales forecast, startup expenses, and break-even analysis. This section mentions how you'll keep the business profitable long term and estimates your profit and loss.

As much as this section estimates revenue, it also estimates your expenses. You need to know what expenses you'll have and how much revenue you need to become profitable. Based on these numbers, what sales goals do you need to meet to be successful? Don't worry too much about the minute details; think in broad strokes. The purpose of this section is to get a rough idea of how your business finances will work. You can refine them later.

Write Your Own Business Plan

Check off the box beside each task as you complete it.

❑ **1. Complete your business plan: 60 minutes**

Download the business plan template at www.The60MinuteStartup.com. Fill out the two-page document. When you're finished, keep it in a safe place so that when the time comes to make iterations, you can do so intelligently.

Daily Standup

Did you complete today's tasks?

- ❑ Yes
- ❑ No

If no, what do you need to carry over to work on tomorrow?

____

What did you learn about your business (or yourself) today that will serve you in the future?

____

Day 14: Location, Logistics, Launch

Coaching for College, Career, and Beyond

Jason Patel is the founder of Transizion, a college- and career-prep platform that connects the best consultants and mentors to high school students, college students, and professionals. Jason is a purple belt in Brazilian jujitsu, a former boxer, and an avid outdoorsman. He brings the same competitive spirit to everything he does. Transizion prides itself on excellent customer service, a 100 percent customer satisfaction rate, and client success.

After graduating from George Washington University, Jason stuck around Washington, DC. He liked the beautiful city and all the buzz surrounding the nation's capital. He wanted to be part of DC's cultural fabric, and he still lives there today. Through college and after, Jason liked helping other students prepare for college prep tests and graduate studies. He volunteered with a lot of students in the DC metro area. These students were mostly from middle-class, lower-income households, and a lot of them were raised by single parents. Jason wanted to help students who needed it and didn't know where to turn. How do you choose a school? How do you enjoy college? How do you choose a major? How do you fill out college applications? What's a good structure for writing a college essay? Jason helped students answer all these questions.

A couple of the students Jason helped did very well in the college application process. One young man earned a full ride to a top school. He studied biomedical engineering to make prosthetic limbs for veterans and children who had lost their limbs in conflict-ridden areas. This student's mother was very grateful for Jason's help, but she cautioned him. She told him that if he kept volunteering his help to students, he would go broke. Then he wouldn't be able to help anyone. She advised Jason to start a business, scale his curriculum, and scale the way he taught students to a larger level.

At the same time, word continued to spread about Jason's ability, and parents started asking Jason to coach their children. The best part? They were willing to pay for his services. So, after a year of volunteering his help, a transition was born. Jason pooled his savings and got a website ready. Jason wasn't tech savvy, so he sought outside help for his website and email marketing. Jason kept experimenting with his business model. Initially, he relied on marketing to career services at colleges and conducting workshops. But Jason realized it was taking forever to get paying students from his efforts. So he ditched that business model and switched to a more one-on-one approach.

Jason realized that parents and students wanted these one-on-one services. He pivoted his strategy to reaching out to parents and students directly. This yielded better results. Jason then hired some freelancers to do digital marketing for his company. Jason also recruited other coaches and mentors who could provide the same services he did to help him expand his business.

As his business grew to support students from across the United States as well as abroad, Jason needed to invest in a phone system, email system, facilities where he could do his coaching, and specific email tools to keep up with his business. Because he has this basic infrastructure, people take Jason and his business seriously.

Today, Jason's team helps students looking to take the next step of their journey. That might be a high school student who needs help with college selection or college applications. Or a graduate student who needs help with the next step in their lives, like deciding whether to go to law school or get a different graduate degree. Jason helps students shine a light on the answers they're looking for. For professionals, that might be a manager or an executive looking to switch jobs or rise up the career ladder. Jason helps them with resumes, cover letters, the interviewing process, their elevator pitch, and networking skills. He connects really smart people with the people who need their help. That's the way Jason adds value to his clients' lives.

Getting Ready to Accept Paying Customers

It's time to get ready to launch your first product or service, which you're going to do very soon. Feel like you're not ready? If you're wondering if you should hold off until it's perfect, you'll be too late. Release your first product, *then* learn how to change it as time moves on. Your first product will never be your last product.

That being said, as you get ready to launch the first product or service of your business, you'll need to make sure you have some necessary infrastructure in place. Like Jason, you'll need an email account, a simple phone system (other than your personal number), a mailing address, and a billing/payment system (even if that system is "cash only").

Can you get by with freely available tools for these basic necessities? Yes, you can! Many entrepreneurs start with Google Duo, Gmail, their home office, and cash/check payments. I started by renting a PO box at a local mail/pack company (like Mailboxes etc.) and getting a toll-free number from Phone.com. Depending on your business, you might need an office setup, some video communication (Skype or Zoom will do, and they're free), and an office or store location to meet clients/customers if necessary.

How do you know what you need to sell your first product? Think through your customer's journey, from the moment they find your business to the close of the sale. A home bakery selling their goods to various retail shops doesn't need an office or a separate mailing address but does need a phone number and an email address to communicate with their customers. If they choose to accept only checks as payment, they don't need to purchase any payment systems. A business consultant may want to rent an office to meet clients, which could also serve as their mailing address. They'll also need a phone number and email address and may want to pay for a simple credit card processor (like Stripe or Square) to accept credit card payments from their clients. Remember, focus only on what you need to get your first paying customer. You can always accept cash or check payments now and invest in a credit card processor down the line.

This is also the time to decide the extent of outsourcing you want to do. Jason relied on freelancers for things like digital marketing and content writing. I relied on freelancers extensively as well. At this point in your business, you may be able to take care of all the things you need. Or you may choose to get some outside help. Some of the common platforms where you can find freelancers are Upwork.com, Guru.com, and Fiverr.com.

Get Ready with Infrastructure: Now It's Your Turn

Check off the box beside each task as you complete it.

❑ **1. Figure out what you need: 15 minutes**

Out of the items mentioned above (email, phone, location, mailing address, and payment system), figure out what infrastructure you need to launch your business. Put checkmarks next to the things you already have in place.

❑ **2. Fill in the gaps: 45 minutes**

Look at the remaining things you need that you don't have in place yet. Get the items and services you need, using free services when possible. At www.The60MinuteStartup.com, I list some commonly used vendors for phone systems, email, et cetera. Use this list to help you fill in your gaps.

Daily Standup

Did you complete today's tasks?

❑ Yes

❑ No

If no, what do you need to carry over to work on tomorrow?

____

What did you learn about your business (or yourself) today that will serve you in the future?

____

60

Day 15: It's Time to Launch

Taking a Side Hustle into a Full-Blown Launch

Jennifer McGinley wanted to be a broadcast journalist like her idol, Katie Couric. During her junior year in college, she interned for an anchorwoman with a television station in Philadelphia. Upon graduation, she shifted to media relations where her talents lay. She worked for other organizations on and off for over twenty years along with consulting. Still, Jennifer wasn't an overnight success. She didn't wake up one day and suddenly have a successful business. Instead, she took the path a lot of first-time entrepreneurs take: she launched her business as a side hustle. A year and a half in, she finally decided to quit her job to work on her business full time.

Today, her company does media relations, community outreach, and reputation management. When she started JLM Strategic Communications, her first gig was doing PR for a nonprofit organization. And she loved it. In fact, she had such a passion for helping industries like health care that she was almost giving her services away for free.

Over time and with practice, Jennifer nailed her process down to a science. First, she found out her client's goals. Then she used those goals to land her media opportunities. As she built credibility for herself and her clients, she used LinkedIn as her go-to platform. That was where she officially "launched" her business when she was ready to take it full time.

Launch Your Business to the Right People

For two weeks, you've been working methodically, building the various pieces necessary for your business launch. But if you think about it, you may have already launched your business. You've been talking to family and friends (hopefully) about your business, getting their advice, validating your ideas, and getting general feedback on various aspects of your business. To some people at least, your business already exists.

Now is the time for the broader launch. Whether you're building a side hustle or a full-blown venture, you want to tell as many people as possible about your business. So how did Jennifer launch her business? She started it as a side hustle, got initial customers from friends and family, and kept her customer pipeline flowing through referrals. Then, when she felt comfortable, she used LinkedIn to let more people know about her business.

Depending on your business model, you'll either use email marketing, social media, or paid advertising to launch your business. Here's a quick breakdown on how to use each.

Email Marketing

If you already have an email list, you can start sending out messages about your business. If you're running promotions, let this list of people know so they can buy from you.

Social Media

It's important to be realistic about social media. You may not be able to publish on every platform every day, so pick the platform most relevant to your target audience. Jennifer started on LinkedIn, but lots of people also launch on Facebook or Instagram.

Advertising

You can buy ads on Google or Facebook to get the word out about your business. If you're running a location-based business, consider ads in local publications. No matter how you get the word out, launching your business also involves engaging your prospects. You can choose CRM (customer relationship management) software or you can use a basic spreadsheet. Track each prospect's name, where they came from, and their level of interest in what you're selling. This way, you can engage with each prospect, find out how motivated they are to buy, and track your sales process with them.

Make Your Launch Happen

Check off the box beside each task as you complete it.

- ❑ **1. Create a graphic with a launch message: 25 minutes**

  Use a free app like Canva to create a fun, easy graphic that announces your business. Write some copy to go along with this image when you share it.

- ❑ **2. Publish on social media: 25 minutes**

  Publish this announcement image and the copy on your favorite social media platforms.

- ❑ **3. Create a prospect tracking list: 10 minutes**

  Start tracking your prospects by creating a list of interested people. Keep track of where they came from, how interested they are in your offer, and whether or not you close a deal with them. Set this up in a spreadsheet or in free CRM software.

Daily Standup

Did you complete today's tasks?

- ❑ Yes
- ❑ No

If no, what do you need to carry over to work on tomorrow?

____

What did you learn about your business (or yourself) today that will serve you in the future?

____

Day 16: Your Customers Are in Social Media Groups—Are You?

Start Small, Start Local, Grow Massive

Zach Hendrix was like any other startup wannabe. He saw the potential of the sharing economy and wanted to take advantage of it. Plus, he had the perfect idea—an app called GreenPal that made lawn mowing easy. People could sign up and get their lawn mowed on the same day even if their grass stood three feet tall. GreenPal was a service homeowners wanted and something to help landscape entrepreneurs grow their customer base. In the long run, it caught on. Zach has over 120,000 customers, 93 percent of whom say they'd recommend GreenPal to a friend.

Sounds easy enough, right? When you're starting out in business, you need leverage to make your idea happen. So Zach did what almost all founders do—he sought funding. He went on the fundraising circuit, talking to angel investors and venture capitalists begging for money to get started. Zach pitched his vision to countless investors but didn't get a penny. Over forty pitches ended in a no.

With one route to funding closed, Zach tried another. He decided to leverage his good credit score to get a business loan. If used right, this loan would be a powerful fulcrum to launch his app into the stratosphere of success. When investors didn't come through, Zach got an $85,000 unsecured line of credit to get GreenPal going (and mowing). That's when things got rocky, fast. Zach burned through that $85,000 loan in his first year. He then had to rely on three cash advances from his personal credit card to keep GreenPal from going under. This additional debt gave Zach a magnifying glass to look at his mistakes. Finally, Zach figured out why the investors he talked to didn't want to give him money.

It was the chicken-and-egg problem. One has to come first, but you can't have one without the other. In the sharing economy, you need both customers and suppliers at the same time. Suppliers don't want to sign up for a platform they're not going to get any gigs from, and customers don't want to be on a platform where there aren't enough suppliers to meet their needs. Plus, Zach's initial app idea was too broad. He promoted GreenPal across North America. When you're trying to be all things to all people everywhere, don't be surprised if you end up being nothing to anyone anywhere.

Watching the near failure of his own business, Zach understood why his business did not deserve outside funding. A lot of locally based sharing economy marketplaces fold when their venture capital runs out. Only money from investors keeps them going, not revenue from customers. A sharing economy marketplace like GreenPal (or Uber) can only keep a tiny percentage of each transaction, so you need loads of customers if you're going to make any money.

Zach had no choice but to nail both supplier and customer acquisition at the same time. He had to get a lot of customers fast. After all, he had massive debts to pay off, he had salaries to pay, and Zach's personal finances were on the line.

Running ads is always an option, but paid traffic to GreenPal wasn't for Zach. Balancing out the cost of customer acquisition versus the small amount he got paid for one transaction was too hard. Instead, Zach decided to focus on unpaid, organic marketing channels. He tried search engine optimization, word-of-mouth referrals in local markets, and media coverage in smaller cities. He also turned to social media, specifically Facebook groups.

The main reason people use social networking apps like Facebook has changed over the years. Today, social media groups are a primary reason people log on to the app. The power of peer-to-peer conversation on a topic of interest? That's hard to find elsewhere. Plus, Facebook users who create groups tend to do a great job of bringing people in the same local area together.

Zach joined local Facebook groups in areas he wanted to grow his app. There he introduced GreenPal to members. By commenting in these groups, Zach ultimately grew his customer base to over 120,000 people. Facebook group success kept his business afloat, but it also let Zach pay off all his debts. By the end of year two in business, Zach had paid back every loan. At the time of writing, GreenPal is in its third year of business and is set to surpass $15 million in revenue.

After growing GreenPal so large through Facebook groups, Zach wanted to find more ways to inject a personal feel into his marketing. So he brainstormed. It turns out the way to a homeowner's heart is through their pets. Now, when a customer signs up for GreenPal, the app asks about any pets so the landscaper will know what to do when they arrive. To customers with pets, Zach sends a personalized gift to the customer's pet. Addressed to the pet, of course.

This new idea took off. Zach's inbox is flooded with personal thank you notes, his social media blows up with mentions, and he can't find enough time in the day to watch videos of dogs chewing on their new toys. For the money Zach invested, this was a huge payoff.

Getting rejected by investors turned out to be a great blessing in disguise. Hard times forced Zach to figure out a way to make things work fast. He didn't want to end up like the many failed sharing economy startups that lean too heavily on investor money to stay in business. Plus, Zach now gets to keep 100 percent of the profit rather than sharing 30 percent, 50 percent, or more with investors.

Zach has been able to help out the small business owners who offer landscaping on GreenPal. For example, one service provider was having a hard time with his own personal finances. Thanks to Zach's successful push to sign up new customers, this landscaper paid off his own debts and caught up with his mortgage payments. The sharing economy is truly all about shared success!

Use Local Social Media Groups to Find Customers

From this chapter onward, this book will teach you a new, unique strategy for getting paying customers. Does it mean you have to implement each one of these fifteen or so strategies? Not really. I expect you to pick a few of these strategies that best suit you and your business and keep working on them. If you realize that the strategies you've picked do not work for your business, pivot and pick a couple of others. Iteration is the core of the agile methodology for building a business.

So now that your business is live, it's time to fill up your pipeline. For that, you need customers. Finding those new customers can be easy, especially with local social media groups on Facebook and other social networking websites.

When Zach joined different local Facebook groups, he monitored the discussions. Anytime someone asked for a lawn care recommendation, he told them about GreenPal in the comments. He tracked link clicks—60 percent of the time Zach recommended GreenPal, a new customer signed up.

You don't need to be in the lawn care business for this approach to work for you. There are Facebook groups in any and every niche you can think of. Once you join a new group, you can immediately jump into the discussions. You can reply to other members' questions, create discussion threads of your own, and give referrals when people ask.

It may take more time than slapping up an ad on Google or Facebook, but group engagement gives you more person-to-person interaction. It shows the group members you're someone they can trust. Plus, Facebook recently launched a mobile app only for groups. The app makes it easy to keep up with posts, comments, and replies in groups you've joined. You can take part in conversations and stay on top of people asking for recommendations without spending hours a day behind a computer.

Your Own Local Facebook Groups Strategy

Check off the box beside each task as you complete it.

❑ **1. Find and join local Facebook groups: 30 minutes**

Log on to Facebook or your favorite social networking app and search for local groups. If you live in a less-populated area, join any and all groups you can find. If you live in a larger city, stick to groups with members in your target audience.

❑ **2. Reply, post, and publish in these groups: 30 minutes**

Scroll through the previous week's conversations. Reply, give advice, and refer your business at any opportunity you see. In groups where it's permitted, write a post telling other members about your offer. No matter what, never talk about religion or politics! Those posts will get you banned faster than other members can block you. Keep it friendly, polite, and professional, and you can expect to find new customers in just about every group you join.

Daily Standup

Did you complete today's tasks?

❑ Yes

❑ No

If no, what do you need to carry over to work on tomorrow?

____

What did you learn about your business (or yourself) today that will serve you in the future?

____

Day 17: Buy Your Own Customers

Born to Be Digital

Digital nomad Ali Saif runs High Clickz, a digital marketing agency. So what's a digital nomad? A digital nomad is someone whose online business doesn't depend on any particular location. Digital nomads can sustain their business from anywhere. Ali's company has a New York City address, but on any given day you can find his virtual office anywhere. Most recently Ali spent two months in Australia for a wedding (and some much-needed rest and relaxation). Because Ali has designed his business to suit his nomadic lifestyle, his business operates smoothly wherever he can find a Wi-Fi connection.

Digital marketing is in demand now more than ever—because entrepreneurs need to find customers online. Not *want*, but *need*. And whenever your target market *needs* your services, you can expect to turn a great profit. In Ali's case, his clients need website traffic that converts into paying customers. For this they might hire a digital marketing agency like High Clickz to develop a lead generation system.

Ali was always destined for the digital world. At a young age, Ali took an interest in computers. He learned computer programming from his uncle, who worked on the computer language Pascal in the 1990s. Ali's uncle took him to technology exhibitions, furthering young Ali's curiosity about all things digital. When Ali got hooked on graphic design and video games as a teenager, his digital destiny was all but sealed. At seventeen, Ali joined a freelance job website and landed his first gig—designing a sales page for a dog-walking training course. He soon landed another project, this time designing a website and developing an online billing system for an internet service provider (ISP) startup.

Ali never looked back. He rode the early 2000s internet trend and won many more freelancing contracts. He then started his own company selling software to ISPs. Four years into this business, Ali shifted his attention to a lifelong passion—online gaming. Ali developed a platform for gamers to play together online. He went on to start gaming teams for Counterstrike and Warcraft championship leagues.

When the economy crashed in 2008, Ali planned and executed a new business model—one that brought in monthly income while helping new business owners get a foothold on the internet. And so High Clickz was born. At that time, not many agencies took advantage of paid advertising. Ali didn't know how to get customers beyond word of mouth and traditional marketing like brochures. But as Google and Facebook came into play, Ali warmed up to online advertising. Ali invested in Google Ads to get his first paying agency clients, who referred more business. These first customers were people who'd lost their jobs and needed to find freelance clients online. He then applied his newfound advertising know-how to help clients implement ad campaigns to grow revenue and increase conversions.

Ali has since expanded to helping small business owners and entrepreneurs reach their full potential online. Specifically, he helps clients use their websites to drive sales, not just to look pretty. The difference between High Clickz and the typical marketing agency is that Ali focuses on measurable results. This way, clients can see how much they're spending on ads and how much they're earning in return. The only reason to try digital advertising is to get paying customers, and that's a lot easier than people think.

A Faster Way to Paying Customers: Paid Advertising

When marketing a business online, "wantrepreneurs" often focus on search engine optimization, beautiful design, guest blog posts, and other approaches to organically growing a business. These work over time. With the right SEO strategy, you'll see results. But there is no faster way to grow your business online than with paid advertising. Platforms like Google and Facebook put your offer in front of customers in *minutes*.

According to research, 65 percent of buyers clicked on ads for a product before they bought it. Paid advertising comes with a 200 percent average return on investment. Sure, the downside is that you need money upfront. But if you're confident about your product or service, and if you can afford to test paid advertising, it's the quickest, easiest way to get your first paying customers. When I ran the pet medicine website, paid ads gave me fast, high return on investment—especially after Google changed their ranking algorithms, and my website dropped from first-page ranking. Paid advertising saved my business.

The most popular paid advertising platforms are pay per click (PPC), meaning you pay the platform every time someone clicks through your ad to your website or landing page. A landing page is a page on your website where customers are presented one offer—buy this product or book this service. You'll be aiming for the best click-through rates (CTR) possible. A good CTR is when a lot of people (10 percent or more) click on your ad. The king of

PPC ads is Google Ads, followed by social media platforms like Facebook. There are other channels, such as influencer marketing, banner advertising, and ad retargeting, that allow you to run ads to people who clicked on a previous ad. For an entrepreneur just starting out, Google Ads and Facebook are your best bets to get a fast return on your investment.

To optimize your ads, I suggest using keywords. When shoppers search for something on Google (like "cheap flea treatment for dogs"), Google presents them with search results that best match their search. If there's a Google ad that uses all or most of the keywords they searched for, that ad will show up first in their search results. So how do you know what your potential customers are searching for? A handy free tool called Google Keyword Planner. This tool tells you how many times people search for certain keywords and phrases. You can find keywords that thousands of people are searching for, incorporate those keywords directly into your ad, then sit back and watch as the clicks roll in.

Once you have a few customers, you can also use ad extensions like Google Reviews to get better CTR. These are reviews your customers have left for you on your Google My Business page. Once you have positive Google Reviews, you can use these reviews in your advertising! (Oh, you don't have a Google My Business Page? Watch a quick step-by-step tutorial at www.The60MinuteStartup.com.)

The Paid Advertising Strategy: Now It's Your Turn

Check off the box beside each task as you complete it.

- ❑ **1. Create Google Ads and Facebook advertising accounts: 15 minutes**

  It's fairly easy to set up your Google Ads and Facebook advertising accounts. Head on over to https://ads.google.com and follow the prompts. Then do the same at https://business.facebook.com. If you need help, hop on www.The60MinuteStartup.com for a detailed tutorial. You can assign a daily amount for each based on your budget. I recommend spending a hundred dollars on each platform per day, but you can spend as little as five dollars per day and still see results.

- ❑ **2. Publish landing pages: 30 minutes**

  Each ad you run (called an ad campaign) should have its own landing page. This way, you can track the effectiveness of each campaign, scaling the ones that work and eliminating those that don't. There are established lead page tools like leadpages.com and unbounce.com to quickly create lead pages. I suggest starting with one ad campaign on Google and Facebook and one landing page where you drive traffic. When you design your landing page, be sure to:

  1. Write your landing page copy to address your customers' needs. Give customers enough information about your product or service to make

a decision. End with a direct call to action (e.g., click here to buy now, click here to book an appointment now, etc.). Your landing page should be one hundred to two hundred words or less. Don't overwhelm customers with a "wall of text."

2. Write a compelling headline for your landing page, appealing to emotions.

- [ ] **3. Create ads: 15 minutes**

Successful advertising is all about relevance. To write winning ad copy that gets people to stop scrolling and start reading your ads, I recommend that you:

- Write persuasive ad copy that aligns with your landing page headline. Your ad copy should be two to three sentences.
- Write a compelling headline for your ad. This is the most important one.
- Head over to Google Keyword Planner at https://ads.google.com/home/tools/keyword-planner and research specific keywords to target (e.g., I targeted "discount pet meds").
- Use ad extensions like Google Reviews to get better click-through rates (CTR). If you have Google Reviews, choose this option when creating your ad on Google. For current ad campaign conversion tips and examples, go to www.The60MinuteStartup.com.

- Adjust your advertising geolocation settings based on specific areas you want to target. Both Google and Facebook will prompt you to do this.
- Optimize your ads for mobile devices. Many if not most people will see your ads on their smartphones. Both Google and Facebook offer a mobile-friendly ad layout when you set up your ad campaign.
- Use remarketing. Both Google and Facebook will offer this as an option for an additional fee. Check www.The60MinuteStartup.com for my latest retargeting tips.

Daily Standup

Did you complete today's tasks?

❑ Yes

❑ No

If no, what do you need to carry over to work on tomorrow?

____

What did you learn about your business (or yourself) today that will serve you in the future?

____

Day 18: When Customers Compete to Work with You

Girls Gone Forex

Robyn Mancell is the cofounder and mind-set coach for Girls Gone Forex, an online trading academy that teaches women across the globe how to trade in the foreign exchange (Forex) market. Forex is the largest financial market in the world, trading $5.4 trillion *every day*. Robyn also runs a nonprofit—Trade Like a Girl Foundation—that empowers women from disadvantaged backgrounds.

Before the Forex business and the nonprofit, Robyn was self-employed for over twenty-five years in several different industries. After her divorce in 1990, she left corporate America, going from stable, salaried nine-to-five employee to a commission-only entrepreneur. All while raising her children as a single mom.

When Robyn started Girls Gone Forex, her only real challenge was that she did not know how to trade. She wanted to find a woman who was a Forex trader. On a trip to Dallas for another business, she met her future business partner, an eighteen-year Forex trading veteran. This woman liked Robyn's new business idea and agreed to be the master trainer at the newly formed Girls Gone Forex.

When Robyn and her business partner first launched the business, they used social media to get the word out. Robyn had been active on Facebook for nine years, so she already had a great following that she'd developed and nurtured. As a result of Robyn's social media activity, women's groups referred people to her. Robyn and her partner became known as "the ladies who teach Forex." Yet posting content on social media about Forex wasn't how Girls Gone Forex landed their first paying customer.

May the Best Forex Trader Win

Robyn's first paying customer found her through a social media contest. Robyn and her partner advertised a free eight-week online class to introduce women to trading. In return for free Forex training, the students would consent to becoming Girls Gone Forex case studies. Over one hundred women applied, competing for the fifteen spots Robyn opened up. She charted all fifteen students' progress over the eight weeks. Once she announced the results of the class and the success of its graduates, Robyn launched the first paid Girls Gone Forex class. A social media post and a press release to local newspapers let women know they were officially open for business. That was March 2017. Since then over two hundred women have gone through Robyn's academy and graduated as successful, profitable Forex traders. What ultimately brought Girls Gone Forex their first paying customers—a social media contest—can help you attract people who become yours.

Social Media Contests: Now It's Your Turn

Check off the box beside each task as you complete it.

❑ **1. Create your social media contest: 15 minutes**

For Robyn and Girls Gone Forex, a social media contest meant competing for a select few spots in her free Forex academy, a program she would later charge for. Maybe you can offer three to five free products, and contestants have to complete an application persuading you, the contest judge, why they deserve the freebies. You could even make your contest go viral. Set a rule that the contestant who publishes their application as an entry and gets more views, comments, or shares than anyone else wins. Get creative and have fun!

- ☐ **2. Monitor contestants' entries: 15 minutes**

  Publish your contest on your favorite social media channel. Ask your friends, followers, and connections to share your contest so that more people enter. I recommend recording a video explaining the rules and the prize so that people don't have to read contest details the length of a short novel.

- ☐ **3. Reward your winner(s): 15 minutes**

  Who earns a spot in your academy? Who gets to try your product for free? Make a big deal about the person! I recommend you judge based on results. If someone shoots a video that gets thousands of shares, you know that person can get noticed online. So when they record a case study or testimonial about your service or product, you can expect their word alone to send actual paying customers your way.

Daily Standup

Did you complete today's tasks?

- ☐ Yes
- ☐ No

If no, what do you need to carry over to work on tomorrow?

____

What did you learn about your business (or yourself) today that will serve you in the future?

____

Day 19: As Featured In

Going Where the Future Is

Nishant Pant is a software architect and a serial entrepreneur with twenty years of experience in the software industry. He has launched five startups in the last decade, some successful, some not. But in his eyes, success is not a destination; it's a journey. So what brought Nishant where he is today is everything he has done in the past combined.

Nishant's latest business is Agent Neo: Voice Technology for Real Estate. With 100 million Amazon Echoes in US households, we are experiencing a paradigm shift in the way we interact with our gadgets. Before you know it, you will be telling Alexa to find someone to mow your lawn or fix your green swimming pool, and Alexa will get it done for you. Agent Neo is currently focused on real estate. Here's how it works. Any person looking to buy or sell a house or just wanting to get a home valuation can download Agent Neo and talk to Alexa about real estate. You can say things like "Alexa, tell Agent Neo to book a home showing on Saturday at seven p.m." Or you could say "Alexa, find me a four-bedroom home in Seattle; my budget is nine hundred thousand." Alexa will then engage you in a quick conversation, collecting all the relevant details from you. The app will then hand you over to a real estate agent in Nishant's network of ten thousand agents countrywide. Think of it as Zillow on voice!

Building a product from just an idea in your head is challenging enough. But what Nishant has learned from his experience is that getting the word out is one hundred times more challenging than creating a product. The popular saying "If you build it, they will come" is not exactly true. In the past, he has built some brilliant products, but he wasn't able to get them where he wanted them; either he wasn't able to get the word out or the word got out so fast that the competition copied the products before he had time to scale. Striking that fine balance has always been Nishant's biggest challenge.

Nishant has tried almost every way to market that you can think of. He's tried Google, Facebook, LinkedIn, and Twitter ads. He has pitched magazines in his niche, contacted influencers and reporters in his city, and hired digital marketers to grow website traffic. You name it, and Nishant has most likely done it. In his opinion, the only marketing tactic that works is one in which you don't pay anybody: specifically, getting covered in an online magazine that is relevant to his domain. Pitching magazines has worked wonders in the past. For Nishant's latest product, he got covered in a reputable real estate magazine the day Agent Neo launched. The story brought hundreds and hundreds of clients in a single day. It was unbelievable. What helped get all the sign-ups was a free beta offer—download the Agent Neo app on the day of release and get free access for a month. Then if you signed up for a paid account, you got a 40 percent discount for the next six months. All these "free" customers became valuable long-term clients.

Get Known, Get Customers

Getting covered in a reputable magazine when you are about to launch is next to impossible. You have to generate some kind of buzz and make it exciting for them. Nishant sent emails to reporters until his fingers bled. He wrote literally hundreds of emails every day. These media pitches were not just copy and paste. He would research reporters who wrote about his niche, find an article written by them, find their email address, and write a personalized email pitching the new product. And 99.9 percent of the time, nobody responded. Frankly speaking, it was very disheartening. But all it took was that 0.1 percent. That did the trick for Agent Neo. And it just might do so for your business too.

How to Get Featured: Now It's Your Turn

Check off the box beside each task as you complete it.

- ❑ **1. Prepare a list of reputable and popular media in your domain: 15 minutes**

  Like Nishant, you can get your business featured in the press. With public relations come customers. What is your target market reading? What magazines do they subscribe to—print or digital? What about blogs or newsletters they subscribe to? Make a list of three to five well-read media outlets you feel you have a good shot at getting covered by.

- ❑ **2. Prepare three to five pitch emails to send to the reporters: 15 minutes**

  I've provided Nishant's outreach emails below. Use these as examples for preparing your own pitches to reporters, journalists, and bloggers.

  Example 1: Share related article email template

  This template will help you share your relevant content related to the journalist's recently published work.

  Subject line: RE: "Real Estate at a Crossroads" article

  Email body:

  Hi, Sally,

Love your writing. I visit your [blog name] blog on [media publication name] very often and especially liked [recent article]. Wanted to share an article that is very relevant to your point.

I saw this hack to find real estate properties easily using Amazon Alexa: [link to article you are sharing].

Interested to know your thoughts. What do you think?

Thanks,

Example 2: Share research specific to the journalist's article

Journalists love data. If you have some research that adds insight to an article they write, you can use this template.

Subject line: Data to support your "Real Estate at a Crossroads" article

Email body:

Hi, Sally,

I have been following your real estate articles for quite some time. Lots of insights indeed.

I couldn't agree more with your assertions in your recent article on "Real Estate at a Crossroads" in [magazine/blog name]. Here are the reasons why:

- Existing home inventory is increasing month to month by 5 percent.
- Number of days in the market has also increased by twenty-five days to thirty-five days.

Our research team has been collecting this kind of data and more using our Alexa-enabled real estate finder app for some time.

Do you think this kind of data is relevant for your audience? Please find the detailed research report attached below.

Regards,

Example 3: Share related article with some provocation template

This example adds some provocation by sharing your relevant article.

Subject line: Voice-enabled real estate search to revolutionize sales?

Email body:

Hi, Sally,

I am a huge fan of your real estate articles on [media/blog name]. I especially liked your most recent article "Real Estate at a Crossroads."

I think the article misses an entirely new way of finding real estate deals—voice-enabled search. As you know, Alexa is one of the top-selling gadgets. More people are using Alexa's search capabilities to easily find real estate deals.

Please check out [your article], which gets into the nuances of this new trend. Your readers may be excited to know about this fast-growing trend.

Thank you,

- ❑ **3. Send your pitches: 30 minutes**

  Good luck! If you don't hear back within a week, be sure to follow up. Write yourself a note if you have to so you remember. Journalists, reporters, and media professionals are busy people. They'll appreciate your follow-up!

Daily Standup

Did you complete today's tasks?

- ❑ Yes
- ❑ No

If no, what do you need to carry over to work on tomorrow?

____

What did you learn about your business (or yourself) today that will serve you in the future?

____

Day 20: Turbocharge Your Referrals Using Social Media

If the Energizer Bunny Was an Entrepreneur

If I had to choose one word to define Adrian Blanco, that word would be *energetic*. Adrian is one of the most passionate, confident, and enthusiastic entrepreneurs I know—bar none. Adrian has been in the jewelry business for twenty years and finally decided to take the plunge to start his own business, Adrian Blanco Jewelry, in 2017.

Why the jewelry business? As a teenager, instead of the typical teenage after-school jobs, Adrian liked the idea of looking professional and wearing a suit. So he applied for a job at a local family-owned jewelry store during his senior year in high school. He rose through the ranks from maintenance clerk to salesperson to jeweler to eventually becoming the store manager.

A few years later, Adrian moved on to a national chain where he could learn another type of retail jewelry. He continued to excel. Even though he was the top salesman, Adrian never felt like he was selling. He simply made relationships. He took a genuine interest in customers' lives. Sales came as an afterthought. His customers trusted him.

While working at that national chain, Adrian started getting discouraged. He didn't like that his job was about numbers rather than people. It didn't sit well with him. So he decided to start his own jewelry business and do things differently. His family hesitated when Adrian shared his plans with them. What if he couldn't get enough customers? Adrian thought about what he was really good at and what he enjoyed. People. Meeting people. Shaking hands. Discovering their stories. Adrian reached out to his network, increased his activity on social media, and started working out of his home. Within one month of doing business on his own, it became apparent that his operation was getting too big for a "home business" operation. Then it was time to open his own brick-and-mortar store.

Adrian knew he couldn't go head to head with other jewelry stores that had much bigger budgets and the ability to advertise. He knew he had to do something different. In his career, he'd noticed that a lot of jewelers didn't do a good job with customer retention. He was always passionate about relationships, making people happy, and making one-to-one connections. So he built those things into his own business. For nearly twenty years, he'd kept in touch with his customers, mostly on social media. He made a vow to himself that he was going to give back to his community as much as it had given him. If he took care of his community, the community would take care of him.

Getting business from his previous clients was easy. But what about getting new customers? Adrian worked with the local Chamber of Commerce and, on his very first day of business, held a grand opening ceremony complete with a ribbon cutting. With very focused advertising to conserve his limited budget, Adrian built his business starting with his earlier clientele, continued using social media in a positive way, and attracted new clients in the process.

Within two years, he'd built great relationships in his local community by giving back as much as possible and also physically meeting as many people as he could and actively participating in organizations like Rotary International. Adrian Blanco Jewelry was selected as the best jeweler in the community twice in a row. Adrian had decided to forego his college education to focus full time on his jewelry career. Instead, he completed courses from the Gemological Institute of America.

Adrian credits a lot of his business success to his ability to keep in touch with people and stay relevant in their lives. Social media has made this so much easier. Can you imagine the old days when people had to send postcards and knock on doors? Adrian is very active on social media. He's always been a positive person, so he posts a lot of positive things. He's a family man, so he often posts pictures of and stories about his family. He also posts about any milestone or award he receives.

Adrian's only regret? He wishes he had opened his own business sooner! He truly believes that "If you like what you do, you'll never work a single day in your life."

Combine Referrals with Facebook

Adrian knew that his strengths were his extensive client network, and his social media accounts (primarily Facebook) that he'd built over the years. Adrian believes his positivity, confidence, and boundless energy also accelerated his business growth.

When it comes to using Facebook to grow your business, what do you do? What should you *not* do? Adrian has some guidelines for you:

1. Adrian's personal brand is a big part of his business. If people know, trust, and buy into Adrian Blanco, they'll buy into his business. Don't be afraid to let your personality shine on social media. People will be more likely to trust you if you show them you're a real person.

2. Always focus on creating and sharing positive posts. Don't just post about your products and services. Post about positive things happening in your community,

with your family, with your customers (with their permission), and anything else you find interesting.

3. Avoid a few controversial topics like politics and religion.
4. Treat every post as a relationship building exercise. Actively communicate with those who like, comment on, and share your posts.
5. Promoting other businesses promotes your own business in the process. Enjoying a glass of your favorite wine? Promote it with a post. Love your car mechanic? Show them your appreciation on social media. This will show your followers that you're a caring consumer as well as a business owner.

Turbocharged Social Media: Now It's Your Turn

Check off the box beside each task as you complete it.

❑ **1. Identify the social media platform that is most appropriate for your business: 10 minutes**

Answer the following questions to identify the best social media platform(s) to use for your business:

1. Are you a business-to-business (B2B) or business-to-consumer (B2C) company? In general, LinkedIn is best for B2B. Facebook, Pinterest, and Instagram are best for B2C. Twitter can be useful for both.
2. Who is your target customer? What platform do they appear on the most?
3. What are your social media goals?

- ❑ **2. Connect with any past clients and references: 30 minutes**

  Take a look at your Rolodex, Google contacts, and phone contacts and start sending friend requests to people you already know. (This should be done from your personal social media account.) Make sure to make your connection requests personal. Don't try to sell anything.

- ❑ **3. Share the exciting news about your new business: 15 minutes**

  Once you've connected with everyone you already know, start posting and sharing the exciting news about your new business. Once again, don't sell anything. Just share.

Daily Standup

Did you complete today's tasks?

❑ Yes

❑ No

If no, what do you need to carry over to work on tomorrow?

____

What did you learn about your business (or yourself) today that will serve you in the future?

____

Day 21: Ninja-Like Conference and Trade-Show Marketing

An Evolving Business Gets Customers in Person

Vivek Kumar had a pretty run-of-the-mill business career. He earned an undergraduate degree from the University of Pennsylvania and got a job at a New York City management consulting firm. Two years later, he switched careers path, landing a job in private equity to get more experience and expand his future prospects.

After four years in private equity and management consulting, Vivek felt called to make a bigger impact on the world. He packed up and moved from New York to Silicon

Valley, where he could work in the booming technology industry. There he got a job selling ads on free Wi-Fi services in public places. Working in sales gave Vivek the motivation and drive to start his own company. He thought that emerging markets would be ideal for the ads-on-public-Wi-Fi business model. Vivek again moved—this time to India. He tinkered with the idea under the first iteration of his company, Qlicket. Everybody told him he had a good product, but a viable market wasn't there. So Vivek pivoted, where instead of providing ads for free Wi-Fi access, he instead utilized the Wi-Fi authentication page to collect feedback from customers. Guests could rate their experience at a given location (instead of posting a bad review on a public website such as TripAdvisor, Google Reviews, or Yelp after the fact), and this information would immediately be sent to someone on staff who could resolve their issues in real time. This worked well in the hospitality industry, where Qlicket grew modestly each month. But this wasn't the bigger impact that brought Vivek into entrepreneurship. He eventually realized that a kiosk-based survey solution could better serve other, larger markets.

Eventually, Vivek's research led him to the employee turnover problem. What he found shocked him—the steep expense of losing one employee and hiring another. How easy could it be to prevent this minimum $50,000 hit to a company's bottom line? Qlicket evolved again. Today, the company caters to blue-collar businesses. Instead of collecting information from customers, his surveys collect feedback from employees. When a company becomes a

Qlicket client, they receive touchscreen kiosks for their workers. These kiosks display workplace announcements and survey questions. Worker responses to these surveys give the management team critical insights about morale and satisfaction. As a result, they can take better care of their workers and, in turn, their families.

What sets Qlicket apart from other survey companies is how their survey method helps management drill down into employee issues. Once employees indicate an area of concern—such as overwhelming workloads—the Qlicket system suggests ways to keep the employee happy and reduce the likelihood of worker turnover. For example, one Qlicket client had a problem with employee turnover, so they used Vivek's kiosks to find out why people kept quitting. It turned out that workers had to stand on their feet for too long, and their legs hurt as a result. The excessive standing was too uncomfortable for some, so they quit without warning and left the company with a void in the workforce.

When management realized the cause of turnover thanks to Qlicket, they let employees vote on a solution. Eventually they bought Dr. Scholl's gel shoe inserts for every employee to help ease the discomfort of standing. The employees felt heard, their foot pain went away, and employee retention increased.

Thanks to Vivek's industry pivot from hospitality to human resources, Qlicket now grows 20 percent month over month. However, during the pivot, Vivek missed payroll for three months and had to lay off some team members. The move from hospitality to human resources rushed Vivek's team to get a product out ASAP even if it was a minimum viable product. Even so, this last iteration could have tanked the business if an investor hadn't stepped in to help.

That investor saved the day, and Qlicket started growing fast and shows no signs of stopping. So how has Vivek found his new clients? He attends manufacturing conferences and trade shows. The strategy is nothing special. Anyone in any industry can buy a ticket and attend a trade show in their niche. To be fair, Vivek has tried other means to find clients like content marketing, search engine optimization, and media coverage. But simply showing up at conferences was the game-changer Qlicket needed. It can be yours as well. And no, it doesn't involve spending a bunch of money to sponsor a booth.

Find Paying Customers at Conferences and Trade Shows

Before attending a trade show, Vivek asked conference administrators for the attendee list. Qlicket sent a cold email to each and every speaker and attendee, offering to take them out for drinks to discuss the employee survey kiosks. For those who weren't initially interested, Vivek followed up with an explainer video featuring the kiosks in action. Since this approach required upfront investment, Vivek did his homework. He researched upcoming events relevant to Qlicket's target market. Only when he knew for sure potential customers would also attend did he buy a ticket.

One of Vivek's cold emails ended up in the inbox of a Fortune 500 executive who managed a large blue-collar workforce. He accepted Vivek's invitation to meet over drinks at a trade show, and they talked for *hours*. Within the week, the Fortune 500 executive signed a contract with Qlicket.

You don't have to develop a specialized product like Vivek to make trade shows and conferences work for you. Vivek's strategy will work for any business model. It doesn't matter if you're a freelancer or you sell products in bulk either. Here's how you can use conferences and trade shows to find your first (or next) paying customers.

Set Up Your Conference Schedule and Start Emailing

Check off the box beside each task as you complete it.

- ❑ **1. Create a list of important conferences and trade shows in your niche: 15 minutes**

  Every niche has important conferences and trade shows. Do a quick Google search and make a list of those that are most important to your customer base. Look for well-known industry leaders and celebrities who are featured speakers. Chances are, that event will attract people with money—people who might just be perfect customers for your business.

- ❑ **2. Select two or three that fit your timeline and budget: 10 minutes**

  Choose two or three conferences or trade shows that are happening soon and near you. Make sure the ticket prices are within your budget. Buy the tickets, put the dates in your calendar, and put a smile on your face. You're about to find customers!

- ❑ **3. Get a list of conference attendees: 10 minutes**

  Go to the conference website, find out who is organizing the thing, and reach out to them via email or social media. Ask for a list of attendees. Some organizers give this list away for free while others ask you to pay for it.

- ❑ **4. Email attendees asking to meet in person: 25 minutes**

  Send out individual emails asking to meet attendees in person. Don't BCC the entire attendee list. Individual emails, personalized messages—these work best. Include a brief note about who your business helps and how in your email so recipients can self-identify that they're a fit for your product or service. It would not surprise me if you make a sale before you ever meet anyone in person.

Daily Standup

Did you complete today's tasks?

- ❑ Yes
- ❑ No

If no, what do you need to carry over to work on tomorrow?

What did you learn about your business (or yourself) today that will serve you in the future?

Day 22: The Premier B2B Sales Engine

Managing Projects, Meeting Presidents, Making Bank

Do digital marketing agencies need a fancy office, long meetings, and a large staff? Not according to Dan Salganik, cofounder and managing partner of VisualFizz, an experiential digital marketing company. VisualFizz is a lean, efficient, risk-loving, experimental agency that works in hot new industries such as e-commerce, health and wellness, construction, and event marketing. Dan has been a serial entrepreneur since his sophomore year in college. Parallel to VisualFizz, Dan runs

Commoot, a machine learning and data company wrapped around a truck advertising platform. Across these companies and some of his past projects, Dan has managed hundreds of team members and run over eight figures in marketing campaigns.

At VisualFizz, Dan oversees the company's strategy and manages client relationships. Dan's skills complement those of his cofounder, Marissa. He has years of project management experience, whereas Marissa's background is in PPC, SEO, and paid and organic social media marketing. So while Dan oversees company growth, client projects, and finances, she manages marketing, operations, and digital implementation. Tasks overlap, as both partners wear many hats on any given day.

Being a marketing agency, VisualFizz serves business clients who need help marketing their products and services. This business model is called business to business, or B2B. Relationship building and referrals are crucial in Dan and Marissa's line of work, so LinkedIn has been an essential part of their social media strategy. Dan posts content promoting VisualFizz on just about all social channels, but around 60 percent of new business comes from LinkedIn. Most inquiries ask about social media advertising, but every once in a while Dan gets an exciting gig. Prior to VisualFizz, one past project involved President Barack Obama, the emperor of Japan, the mayor of Chicago, and Yoko Ono, widow of Beatles legend John Lennon. Dan worked with drone specialists to take aerial footage of Chicago South Side parks for a documentary portraying the area's renewal. Near the Obama Library is the Phoenix Pavilion, a gift from the

Japanese government over one hundred years ago. The pavilion fell into disrepair and burned down. Dan's project captured the rebuilding effort to open a new-age Phoenix Pavilion dedicated to the Japanese-American relationship. The documentary not only built a stronger alliance with the Japanese government, but also led to thousands of new jobs, updated park systems, improved infrastructure, and the upcoming grand reopening of the Phoenix Pavilion.

Without LinkedIn, Dan and Marissa would not know about some amazing high-visibility opportunities. If Dan can find work with celebrities and world leaders, surely you can use LinkedIn to get your first paying customer!

Getting B2B Customers: The LinkedIn Strategy

LinkedIn is the internet's largest professional network, with more than 500 million members in over two hundred countries. According to research, 94 percent of B2B marketers distribute content on LinkedIn, and 74 percent of B2B buyers use LinkedIn for purchasing decisions. I recommend you use LinkedIn to find potential prospects, make connections, and build relationships like Dan and Marissa have. Then move the dialogue beyond LinkedIn to close the sale.

Find Potential Prospects: LinkedIn has excellent search capabilities with specific filters to zero in on prospects. Some search filters are available based on your membership level. For example, Sales Navigator, a premium feature, offers a robust set of filters for highly targeted searches. For new entrepreneurs, the free basic membership is all you need.

Make Connections: Send your targeted prospects a connection request. Attach a personalized message to every request, an option LinkedIn offers before you connect. Give prospects a reason they should connect. What's in it for them?

Build Relationships: Once your prospects connect with you, start a dialogue. How? What do you say? Share content they might find valuable. Make sure your conversations are not perceived as a naked sales pitch. That's the surest way to kill any budding relationship, online or off. Ask yourself these questions when deciding what content to share:

- What are they interested in?
- What is important to them?
- What problems do they face?

Move Conversation Offline: Once you've got a chat going and you've built initial trust, take the relationship offline either via a phone call, a video call, or an in-person meeting. More often than not, connections become clients through offline interactions rather than on LinkedIn itself.

The Link to Paying Customers: Now It's Your Turn

Check off the box beside each task as you complete it.

❑ **1. Use LinkedIn search to find prospects: 30 minutes**

Search for prospects based on their job title, their company, or a group they've joined. If you don't know what common job titles your target market has or which companies they work for, check out LinkedIn groups where they may hang out. For example, Dan and Marissa would join digital marketing support groups where business owners go to share social media marketing tips. Any and all members are potential prospects.

- [ ] **2. Send connection requests: 15 minutes**

Once you've found the right type of people, reach out to fifteen prospects. Write a message explaining how you believe you can help the prospect out for free, perhaps through an article you've written or useful study you came across. Personalize this connection message when you make each request so that you're addressing each prospect by name. Check out www.The60MinuteStartup.com for connection request message examples sure to get prospects replying to you right away.

- [ ] **3. Prepare follow-up message plan for subsequent conversations: 15 minutes**

If only one prospect accepts your LinkedIn connection request, that's one potential customer you should treat like royalty. Use the free follow-up message templates at www.The60MinuteStartup.com to build rapport, establish your credibility, and invite the prospect into a face-to-face conversation, whether that's via video conference or in person.

Daily Standup

Did you complete today's tasks?

❑ Yes

❑ No

If no, what do you need to carry over to work on tomorrow?

____

What did you learn about your business (or yourself) today that will serve you in the future?

____

Day 23: Want Customers? Borrow Someone Else's

From $1.67 an Hour Writing Gigs to #1 Bestselling Ghostwriter

When Joshua Lisec started his freelance writing business in 2011, he hoped to one day quit his full-time cubicle job, build a multiple six-figure business while traveling the world, and employ his future spouse so they could work and raise children together. But Joshua's first writing gig paid a mere $1.67 an hour.

Joshua quickly pivoted from writing articles and web content under his own name to ghostwriting, a type of professional writing where the writer creates content in the voice of the client, who gets the credit.

That pivot changed everything. Along with contracts to write direct response sales copy and build online product launch funnels, Joshua now ghostwrites thought leadership books and *Forbes* articles for award-winning business owners, chief executives, coaches, consultants, inventors, investors, multimillionaire and billionaire serial entrepreneurs, philanthropists, politicians, and religious leaders. Joshua has ghostwritten over forty full-length nonfiction books and novels. He is also the first Certified Professional Ghostwriter in Ohio.

Joshua offers his clients a unique book writing and publishing experience. First, he focuses on author voice authenticity, using writing analytics software to study and recreate an author's writing style and tone. As a result, every manuscript reads as if the author themselves wrote it.

Second, Joshua gives authors multiple paths to create return on their investment. His strategies help authors convert readers into clients through a combination of book marketing funnels, paid speaking opportunities, major media appearances, and corporate sponsorship.

Third, Joshua goes beyond the typical "pay me to write a Word document" ghostwriting with a special service called "ghostpublishing." As with ghostwriting, Joshua and his team do all the work so authors can sit back, sell books, and cash royalty checks.

Joshua's success as a ghostwriter has landed his company, www.EntrepreneursWordsmith.com, big media appearances with American Express, BBC Radio London, Fatherly, Foundr, Freelancers Union, the *Huffington Post*, the Nonfiction Authors Association, *The Side Hustle Show*, TED, TEDx, the Write Life, Yahoo!, and others. Best of all, he fulfilled his dream of quitting his full-time job, growing his business to multiple six figures, and working alongside his wife, Judy Shaw, while they raise their son Wesley. And yes, they've traveled abroad while working on laptops.

In a profession where "good" ghostwriters earn a few hundred dollars on freelance marketplaces, Joshua makes $35,000 to $100,000-plus per project. He also charges premium prices for article and web content ghostwriting. For both types of services, Joshua has found unique ways to attract clients, one of which he calls the **Other People's Audience (OPA) Strategy**.

A Faster Way to Paying Customers: The OPA Strategy

Unlike the freelance marketplaces he used to build his business in the early years, the OPA Strategy positioned Joshua as the only professional ghostwriter to consider. No competition! In contrast to social media and email marketing, this strategy allowed him to tap into other people's audiences to find and close new clients. Here is how the OPA Strategy works.

Joshua connected with local noncompeting business owners who serve the same target market he does. For example, Joshua ghostwrites for entrepreneurs. Who else has entrepreneur clients? Certified public accountants. So Joshua approached CPAs in his area and asked if their clients experienced a specific problem—online marketing that didn't convert. If they said yes, he made an offer: "I'll teach your clients something new to grow their business, make you look good, and buy everyone lunch. Deal?"

Local accounting firms agreed to host Joshua's "lunch and learns" and spread the word to their business owner clients. In return for showing up, Joshua gave business owners a free presentation with helpful advice on growing their businesses. Joshua used a basic slideshow template. He talked about why most content marketing campaigns don't work and what to do about it.

Every workshop was a hit! The accountant won because the presentation got their clients back through their doors, which led to repeat business. The clients won because Joshua's free presentation helped fix their broken marketing. And Joshua won because he positioned himself as the go-to ghostwriter. The first two times Joshua used the OPA Strategy, he spent $250 on lunch but closed almost $10,000 in web content ghostwriting work. Pretty good return on investment!

So how exactly did Joshua walk out of these firms with sales without being salesy? First of all, Joshua provided free, valuable information. In his presentation, Joshua included portfolio excerpts and testimonials to prove his advice had worked for others. And instead of closing his presentations with a pitch, Joshua said, "If I could demonstrate a process to you where you're able to achieve the results you want, are you open to chatting more? If so, come up, and we'll put a time on our calendars."

There you have it. With Joshua's OPA Strategy, you can stop struggling to get noticed as a small fish in a big pond. Now you're not only the big fish, you're *the* fish!

The OPA Strategy: Now It's Your Turn

Check off the box beside each task as you complete it.

- [ ] **1. Create your presentation title: 5 minutes**

  What problem does your product or service solve? What goals do you help customers achieve? Use one of these headline formulas to give your presentation an exciting title. Which formula you pick doesn't matter. The agile way is all about speed over perfection. Pick the first formula you like, fill in the blanks with your business, and move on to step two.

  - Could ______________________ Be Keeping You from ________________________?
    - *Ex: Could Your Social Media Pages Be Keeping You from Attracting Customers?*
  - Everything __________________ Need to Know about __________________

   - *Ex: Everything Physical Therapists Need to Know about Vitamins and Supplements*
- __________? Do THIS First.
   - *Ex: Thinking about Adopting a Rescue? Do THIS First.*
- How to __________ in __________ or Less
   - *Ex: How to Build a Profitable E-Commerce Website in Seven Days or Less*
- Learn How to __________ over Free Lunch
   - *Ex: Learn How to Grow Your HVAC Business Online over Free Lunch*
- __________ Ways to __________ Even if __________
   - *Ex: 7 Ways to Increase Your Home Value Even if You're Not a Professional Remodeler*
- __________ Secrets to __________
   - *5 Secrets to Finding Better Tenants for Your Rental Properties*
- Why __________
   - *Why Every Real Estate Agent Should Use Social Media*
- How to __________ (Without __________)
   - *How to Lose Ten Pounds This Month (Without Cutting out Your Favorite Foods)*
- __________ Easy Steps to __________
   - *Four Easy Steps to Going Vegan*

- [ ] **2. List your key presentation points: 5 minutes**

How are you going to deliver what your presentation promises? Take a few minutes now to write down five to ten key steps, tactics, or tips that will allow your audience to digest your advice while digesting lunch. For example, if your presentation is "Seven Easy Ways to Keep Pests out of Your Garden," write down those seven easy ways below. No, you don't need a word-for-word script. Just write down a few keywords related to each way to keep a garden pest-free. List your key presentation points in the space provided below:

____

____

____

____

____

- [ ] **3. Design your presentation slideshow: 10 minutes**

You don't need a fancy slideshow or beautiful handouts designed by a graphics professional. All you need is a free PowerPoint, Google Slides, or Slideshare template. Put your presentation title on the cover slide. Give each key presentation point its own slide with one accompanying photo. I recommend going to free stock photo websites like Unsplash, Pixabay, and Wikimedia Commons. Your presentation is ready in minutes.

If your OPA host does not have a projector, you can set up your own mini projector. All you need is a blank, light-colored wall and a portable mini projector that plugs into your laptop or smartphone. I recommend the Meyoung Portable Projector and GooDee Mini Projector. At the time of publication, both are available on Amazon for $49.99. See my latest recommendation at www.The60MinuteStartup.com.

- [ ] **4. List your potential OPA hosts: 5 minutes**

Who do you know that already serves your future customers? For example, Joshua knew several accountants, whom he reached out to via email. If you don't know any small business owners or professionals targeting the same market as you, ask a friend or family member who they do business with. Then ask for an introduction. Write down three to five potential OPA hosts in the space provided below:

____

____

____

____

____

- [ ] **5. Write your OPA host email pitch: 5 minutes**

In Joshua's outreach to accounting firms, he included two messages in a single email. One, a pitch for the OPA opportunity. Two, a pitch for the presentation itself. The first half of the email explained how the presentation would benefit the accounting firm. The second half invited the firm's clients to the presentation. If the firm said yes, their executive assistant could simply copy, paste, and send that invitation to the firm's clients. Below is a template for your OPA pitch based on the exact email Joshua used to book lunch and learns and score big clients. Tweak the email script as necessary.

Hi __________,

Congratulations on your recent successes at ________!

__________ recommended that I reach out to you. He and I have been talking recently about a lunch and learn workshop centered around __________. Have your clients told you about struggles with __________? I thought __________ might be something your clients would like to hear about over a free meal.

Do you agree that a lunch and learn on _______ would be of value to your clients? They'll learn something new about __________, and they'll be grateful because you looked out for their best interest.

If this sounds like a yes or maybe, take a look at this draft email inviting people to the free workshop:

* * * *

Hello [recipient],

I'm reaching out to you because we are hosting a lunch and learn on [topic]. It's called [your presentation title].

[Your title and name] let us know about a sobering statistic:

[A statistic that proves the need for your product or service].

Because of [comment on the statistic and give your opinion of how it affects your potential customers].

While you enjoy a free lunch, [your name] will be showing you how to:

- [your key presentation points]
-
-
-
-
-

If you want to stop [a problem your product or service solves] and [a benefit of working with you], please call our office at __________ to reserve your spot.

* * * *

If this looks like a go, let me know the best date in [month] or [month] to get this lunch and learn on your schedule.

All the best,

____

- [ ] **6. Order boxed lunches: 10 minutes**

NOTE: You will complete steps six and seven on the day of the presentation itself. Obviously, I'm not expecting you to complete all seven steps today. It may take a few days or a week to hear back from your potential OPA hosts and schedule your presentation. Do everything you can now and finish the final steps as you book your lunch and learns.

Give your presentation's attendees a respectable lunch. Fast-casual fare is fine; fast food is not. When Joshua used the OPA Strategy, the CPA firms' executive assistant took each guest's lunch order when they called to reserve their spot. You don't have to get that personal. All you need is a rough estimate of the number of attendees so you know how many boxed lunches to order. Don't forget to buy one for yourself!

- [ ] **Deliver your presentation and get customers: 20 minutes**

Dress business casual. Test your projector and presentation as soon as you arrive. Greet everyone with a firm handshake, give each guest their lunch, and ask them to hold any questions until the end. To get the ball rolling, ask everyone what they hope to take away from the presentation. You might keep those expectations in the back of your head so that you fulfill them in your talk.

You'll probably feel nervous, and nerves make you talk faster. So deliver your presentation at a slower speed than feels normal. Slowing down will also help you keep the uhs and ums to a minimum. Smile and talk to your audience, not to your slides. Keep your talk to fifteen minutes so that you don't risk people getting bored and leaving early to get back to work.

When you close, use Joshua's closing invitation:

If I could demonstrate a process to you where you're able to achieve the results you want, are you open to chatting more? If so, come up, and we'll put a time on our calendars.

Daily Standup

Did you complete today's tasks?[6]

- ❑ Yes
- ❑ No

If no, what do you need to carry over to work on tomorrow?

____

What did you learn about your business (or yourself) today that will serve you in the future?

____

[6] Bookmark this page and come back to check off the yes box when you've completed steps six and seven.

Day 24: Fill Job Vacancies without Going Back to a Cubicle

When New Customers Hide in Plain Sight

Alwi Suleiman's story began in Mombasa, Kenya. He was a bright, determined twenty-two-year-old. Alwi wasn't an entrepreneur, but he felt determined to make enough money to improve his mother's and siblings' standard of living. So Alwi got a full-time job with zero days off. He worked six full days every week and half a day on Sundays. The job paid off—Alwi bought a (secondhand) car that he used as a taxi and a four-bedroom mud house, which he rented out for extra income.

After moving to the Netherlands, the status quo kept Alwi happy for two decades. But by his early forties, he'd decided to break out of the golden cage that was a comfortable office job. In the internet age, Alwi had become a digital marketing expert. Alwi took a leap like the one you've taken—he started his own business, Content Market King. Today, Alwi helps small businesses save time and money with smart content marketing strategies and campaigns. As an experienced marketer, Alwi knew content needed to be at the heart of every marketing strategy, especially for small businesses. Content is king, after all!

Alwi's doctrine is "Marketing is about help and not hype. Your audience must believe that you're there to help solve their problems and tend to their needs." The desire to help has to be clear in all the content he helps his clients create. It doesn't matter which marketing platform they use, the type of content they publish, or who their audience is.

Meanwhile, Alwi found it hard to find time to get started. He was a father of three with a day job. Entrepreneurship demanded his nights and weekends. Life got a little lonely—the usual price to pay to become your own boss. For Alwi—and for you since you've made it this far—that price is worth it.

To grow his side business, Alwi chose not to spend money on ads. Instead, he got creative in his search for clients. He ended up on the LinkedIn job board. He already used the social media networking site to make business contacts, but something urged Alwi to look at the job listings. Alwi swears it's one of the most underrated ways to find customers. In fact, that's how he got his first paying customer—and how you might find yours.

Using Job Vacancies to Land Client Deals

When you're starting out, you have to put yourself out there. You have to sell yourself. And you have to be able to convince people looking for in-house professionals that what you offer is more valuable than a full-time hourly or salaried employee. Alwi did exactly that. To this day, he prefers to use LinkedIn to network instead of investing in advertising. He's built up a LinkedIn business page with over two hundred followers to help him reach even more people, but you don't need that to get started. All you need is a few minutes to search the job listings. If you offer a service like consulting, copywriting, or search engine optimization, you will probably find open jobs in sixty seconds or less.

In the case of Alwi's first client, he responded to a job listing with his resume. He received a rejection letter, which gave him an idea. Alwi wrote back, offering himself as a freelancer for any future needs. A few weeks later, the company got back in touch and asked him if he could take on some work for them. Alwi accepted. See? Landing a paying customer doesn't have to be rocket science.

Land Your Own Gigs from Job Listings

Check off the box beside each task as you complete it.

❑ **1. Search for job vacancies: 15 minutes**

Use LinkedIn or another popular job board like Indeed or Monster to search for both full-time and contract job vacancies. Make a list of five to ten that you'd be well suited for, given your work experience, resume, and strengths.

❑ **2. Send emails: 45 minutes**

Send emails to the hiring manager letting them know you're available for hire as a freelancer. Some listings give special instructions to follow when sending emails. Follow them so that your application doesn't get ignored. Remember, if the company gives the job to someone else, you can always do what Alwi did. Offering yourself as a freelancer in the future causes no harm. Plus, it gives you new potential clients in your pipeline.

Daily Standup

Did you complete today's tasks?

❑ Yes

❑ No

If no, what do you need to carry over to work on tomorrow?

____

What did you learn about your business (or yourself) today that will serve you in the future?

____

Day 25: Going Where Your Customers Already Are

When Entertainers Make the Best Entrepreneurs

Rio Rocket became an entrepreneur at age six when he sold his first comic book to his cousin for twenty-five cents. Rio began his career as a part-time graphic artist and web designer in the early stages of the modern internet. His passion for graphic design evolved into a full-service commercial graphic art, web development, and digital marketing service.

But Rio was always looking for new and different ventures. Rio entered acting as a voice artist. After performing all the male character voices for *The Trials of Olympus* video game and twelve different voices for the feature film *Heartlock*, Rio moved to film and television, taking gigs as a commercial model, motivational speaker, event host, presenter, and even a motion-capture athlete. From the start of his first business, Rio flowed through multiple careers as an entrepreneur without skipping a beat. These days, Rio still wears the hat of branding and visual design expert while maintaining a thriving acting career, even putting these skills to work for his own acting brand. His skill set includes not only branding but also maintaining a high level of brand awareness long after the branding process is complete. He increases brand visibility and social vibrancy for his clients, using online and offline marketing as well as television and film.

When starting each new venture, Rio took on the challenge of getting clients and customers—even with little or no experience in that field. When he began as a graphic artist, Rio grew his business on the Elance.com platform. Working for modest rates and doing work pro bono was key to developing a strong portfolio in the early stages of his career. If you love what you do like Rio, you'll advance through this stage quicker than you might expect.

Pitch, Price, Portfolio—The Three Ps to Get Your First Customers on Freelance Job Websites

When you're not an established entrepreneur, getting your first paying clients can take a bit of creativity and persistence. When Rio began his graphic art and web development business, he secured his first client by creating a profile on Elance.com (now Upwork.com). He learned how to craft a **professional pitch** to bid on design projects and used strategic **pricing** to secure his first logo design client.

Your pitch and pricing are everything in the early stages when you don't have client reviews yet. By securing work (even for a low fee or for free) right away, you can build a **portfolio**, which acts as proof for prospective customers. The right client will give you a chance if you display your ability to get the job done at a price that offsets any risk of working with an unseasoned vendor.

So what exactly is a portfolio? If you're a freelance writer, your portfolio is made up of samples of previous content you've written. If you're a consultant, it's filled with one-page write-ups of successful case studies. Web designer? Take screenshots of previous websites you've built. What if you don't have a portfolio? If you're just starting out, what can you use in the meantime while you build one? If you don't have pictures, articles, or case studies, then you can turn your resume or CV into a portfolio. For every accomplishment or skill that you list, create an infographic using www.Canva.com. Then upload those graphics in place of a standard portfolio.

After growing his initial customer pipeline, Rio can now rely on referrals and word of mouth to keep his business growing. But when he was just starting out, he crafted the following pitches and posted them on Elance to get his first paying clients in each of his niches:

Rio's Branding Pitch Script

> Greetings! We are committed to the output of high-quality service in the areas of graphic design, logos, illustrations, and advertisements. We are a boutique that caters to our customers' individual needs without the big-name agency price tag. No matter how simple or intricate the task, your project, your satisfaction, and our diligence are guaranteed. We have completed projects for individuals, as well as for small, midsize, and large companies. Our commitment is to deliver top-quality design to your specification and, most importantly, do so on time.
>
> We realize your image means everything, and your design needs a flair to set yourself apart from the mainstream. Allow us the opportunity and privilege to work on your project, and we will turn your ideas into images. Fifty percent deposit on agreed pricing or estimate for project.
>
> The balance will be paid upon completion of project, and then all copyrights on design are turned over to the client.
>
> Rapid turnaround!
>
> Unlimited revisions within project scope are included at no additional cost to client. Final work will be delivered in the format of your choice for the flat fee of the bid

amount. 100 percent satisfaction is guaranteed. We will make your dreams spring to life!

Rio's Graphic Design Pitch Script

Greetings! Why should you choose us for the job? We produce professional graphics to increase your visibility among the mediocrity of mainstream design while providing only the highest level of service.

Please review our portfolio for samples and open a dialogue through a private message board for further discussion. We look forward to working with you.

Rio's Website Design Pitch Script

Meet a highly qualified, experienced, and ultra-creative designer that will enhance your web presence to the power of 10 and beyond. We develop secure, optimized, and cutting-edge institutionalized web sites using the latest programming and design technology. Above all, we take the time to research your demographic and understand your business and its philosophy. We also offer "around the clock" responsiveness before, during, and after the development phase. An enhanced web presence with all the bells and whistles according to your requirements is yours with bid acceptance.

Please review our work process and portfolio for samples and open a dialogue through a private message board for further discussion. We all look forward to working with you.

Pitch on Upwork: Now It's Your Turn

Check off the box beside each task as you complete it.

❑ **1. Craft your pitch to post on Upwork: 20 minutes**

Using one of the examples above (or crafting your own unique pitch from scratch), write your pitch for your profile on Upwork. It should be about 125 words and passionately convey the commitment you'll offer your clients.

❑ **2. Pick your price point: 20 minutes**

Decide what minimum price you will accept as you start your new business, build your portfolio, and make yourself visible. If you don't get a client within one week of publishing your profile, lower your price or offer services for free for a limited time. Remember, the objective is to gain work experience, satisfied clients, and a nice portfolio so you'll land higher-paying clients in the near future.

❑ **3. Complete your Upwork profile with your portfolio: 20 minutes**

Go to Upwork.com. Complete your profile and upload your pitch and your portfolio or infographics.

Daily Standup

Did you complete today's tasks?

❑ Yes

❑ No

If no, what do you need to carry over to work on tomorrow?

What did you learn about your business (or yourself) today that will serve you in the future?

Day 26: Bartering—The Oldest Way to Get Customers

Anjana Wickramratne started out as a graphic designer. Unfortunately, Anjana's graphic design website wasn't getting any visitors. While trying to figure out why, Anjana stumbled upon digital marketing. Anjana quickly fell in love and started his own marketing agency—Inspirenix—to help businesses find customers online. Inspirenix helps small and large businesses of every kind get more exposure through Google searches, develop their websites, grow on social media, and sell via email. What makes Anjana's agency remarkable is where and when he started Inspirenix—he started building the agency on the Asian island of Sri Lanka when he was just sixteen years old. As you can imagine, young Anjana faced a few challenges. First, he needed to get his first client. Then he had to manage and grow his business as well as recruit new employees with the right skills. On top of all that, Anjana had well-established digital marketing agencies to compete with to get customers.

After Anjana landed his first paying clients in a unique way (more on this in a moment), he search engine optimized his website to rank better on Google. Anjana didn't do a lot of advertising. He ran a few Facebook and Instagram promotions for a small amount—and that was it. Instead of tons of ads, Anjana focused on growing his business with social media engagement. He shared informative posts on social media and created valuable content that others could benefit from. Anjana found that he had more of a personal touch than his competitors. It was more effective to engage with real people than to run paid promotions. This allowed him to create a community around his business.

At the start of his digital marketing agency, Anjana struggled a lot to get his first paying client. Anjana did tons of research and even reached out for advice from other established agencies in his niche. Then Anjana did something different. He contacted a business outside his industry that already had clients that could use his digital marketing services.

Anjana contacted a graphic design agency that built brand images for their clients. He asked if they would send their clients to Inspirenix after their images were complete so Anjana could help them grow their brand online. But Anjana knew the graphic design agency wouldn't be interested in giving referrals to him for free—so he offered them a proposal. He offered his digital marketing services to the graphic design agency for free to boost their ranking online. In return, they agreed to send Anjana potential clients. A win-win situation!

To execute Anjana's idea, the graphic design agency sent a message to their existing clients about his services. That's what got Anjana his first paying client. History buffs like me are fascinated by the fact that bartering—trading products or services with someone else—was the world's first customer acquisition method. Thousands of years before currency existed, hunter-gatherers traded food and tools with others to survive. If bartering worked for our ancient ancestors, why can't it work to help you get your first paying customer?

Today Anjana's digital marketing agency, Inspirenix, has over a thousand clients from all over the world. That wouldn't have been possible if he hadn't used this technique to get his first paying client. To get additional clients, he also sent cold emails to the graphic design agency's customers. Take a look at one of these emails below, as well as the email Anjana sent to the graphic design agency:

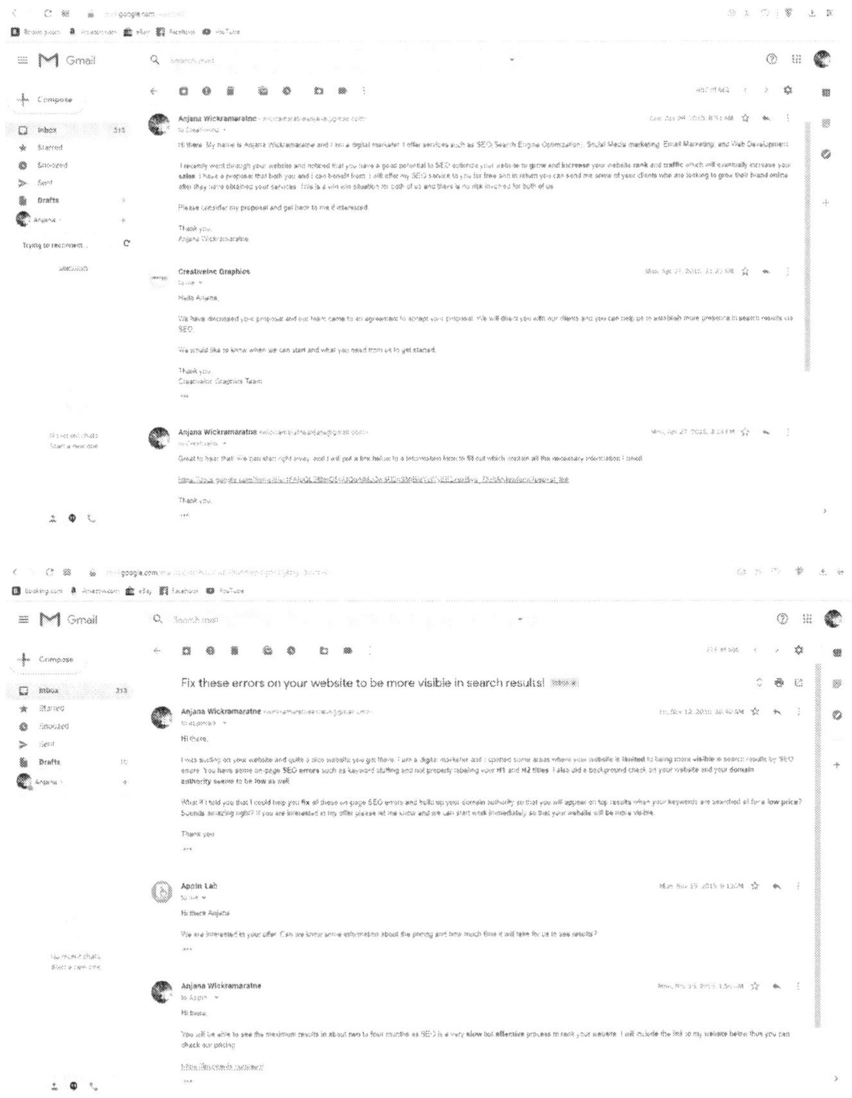

Trading Customers

So how do you achieve the same success that Anjana enjoyed? How do you find other companies to partner with that are already serving your ideal clients? Think about the people you want to sell your products or services to. What other services are these people likely already paying for? If you're a plumber, that might be an electrician or a contractor. If you sell vintage clothing, that might be a stylist or a designer shoe retailer.

Once you've identified what types of businesses to contact, think about what kind of trade you could offer. Try to stick with bartering services rather than paying for referrals. If you're a yoga instructor, offer free classes or private sessions to the staff. If you sell handmade items, offer free, discounted, or custom pieces. If you can't find a business to barter with, offer a 5 percent referral fee for every client they send you—payable after the client has paid *you*, of course!

Get Referrals: Now It's Your Turn

Check off the box beside each task as you complete it.

❑ **1. Research potential businesses to barter with: 30 minutes**

Identify what type of businesses to reach out to. Which industry? And where? Got it? Great. Now google around and find three to five individual businesses to contact.

❑ **2. Craft an email for trading services: 20 minutes**

Using Anjana's emails as your inspiration, craft your message to reach out to potential trading partners.

❑ **3. Send emails to businesses: 10 minutes**

Tailor the email you crafted to each of the businesses you found in your research and send.

Daily Standup

Did you complete today's tasks?

❑ Yes

❑ No

If no, what do you need to carry over to work on tomorrow?

____

What did you learn about your business (or yourself) today that will serve you in the future?

____

Day 27: Proving Your Product

Bare, Beards, and Better Skin Care

Skin care is not just a woman's thing anymore. So says Rin Gamache, a licensed esthetician and wellness entrepreneur. Her men's skin care product line—Bare & Beards—helps men with acne, razor bumps, ingrown hairs, and aging. Rin herself suffered from acne as a teen and an adult. As a young woman, how she looked weighed heavily on Rin's self-confidence. She didn't go to parties or networking events. She did see a dermatologist, who prescribed temporary relief antibiotics. But prescription drugs did more harm than good, scarring Rin's face. Her dermatologist wanted Rin to take Accutane, the closest thing to a cure, according to drug companies. Debilitating side effects include scarring and also severe joint and muscle pain. So Rin went on her own journey to figure out a safer, gentler skin care solution.

Soon Rin found an online forum where other women discussed everything from natural remedies to fight acne to common household chemicals that trigger flare-ups. These posts inspired Rin to try natural products on her skin. It was trial and error until she found the right combination. She became passionate about skin care. When you struggle with skin issues, you always focus on other people's skin, Rin realized. She noticed how her male friends and family members with skin issues just let their skin be. They had zero clue about identifying their skin type, let alone which products to use. So she decided to invest in her passion—esthetics school. She wanted to become an expert and use her background in sales and marketing to go after the male demographic. These men needed a skin care education that no one was offering. And Rin was up to the challenge.

When she first developed her skin-care line, she tried everything. She introduced herself to men at barbershops and salons who she believed could benefit from her products and services. She also set up a vendor booth at barbering shows, sporting events, and pride parades. She handed out business cards and asked select men to try her products at no cost. The barber trade shows worked well for Rin. Barbers either ordered her natural skin-care products wholesale or bought a few bottles on the spot to try. Sporting events and pride parades didn't work out.

Rin noticed that the men who needed her products most got so self-conscious when they saw her booth, they hurried past without stopping.

Rin also tried paid promotions on social media. Those worked a little. Two customers who saw her sponsored post advertising Bare & Beards ended up giving her their business. She then switched from social media ads to sponsorship. Bare & Beards sponsored a beard cam for a local pro-am hockey team during the playoffs. Her logo appeared on the Megatron, and she received in-arena messaging. Expensive and unsuccessful. Next up came Groupon, a website and app that connects subscribers with local businesses by offering discounts on products and services. Rin found several one-time customers on Groupon, but they were all deal chasers. Only one customer repurchased Bare & Beards products from her online store.

How Rin Sold Customers on Her Product (Then Actually Sold the Product)

What worked better than anything was Rin's outreach to barber colleges and product demos. Rin asked barber college instructors if she could offer skin care presentations and how-to demos on how to sell Bare & Beards products. Several colleges said yes, and, as you're about to find out, the rest is skin-care history.

She went to barber colleges to give presentations on the importance of implementing skin care in their barbering services and learning about product ingredients and benefits to be able to sell products. She gave a skin-care demo using her product. The students ended up purchasing her product to practice selling to their clients while in school. So this was successful because not only was Rin educating them, she was also promoting her product. Some students bought.

Rin also gave away free skin-care treatments to a few men to help promote her clinic. She wanted to use them as models to perform certain services for before and after photos so she could show how using skin care therapies regularly would help improve said skin conditions (acne, scarring, fine lines, etc.). She would also learn how to price her services. Rin found these clients by going out and getting them. If she saw men with skin issues at a gas station or at the supermarket, she asked them to be a model for her new clinic. But they needed to commit to it for six consecutive weeks. Rin sent them home with her Bare & Beards 4-in-1 Daily Cleanser during the testing phase, so she knew her product would do what she said it would do. Rin took progress photos to use in advertising and marketing to show how her products and services provided a solution to men's skin issues. After the six weeks was up, two men turned into regular paying customers.

Rin is running her demo again, helping more men improve their skin, and she's showcasing their before and after photos to educate and convert even more new customers. Like Rin, you can find future customers to demo your product or service, prove it does what you say it can, then convert those people into paying customers or promote their results to find new customers.

Demos: Now It's Your Turn

Check off the box beside each task as you complete it.

❑ **1. Identify who can use your product or service: 15 minutes**

By use, I mean really, *really* use your product or service. Rin wanted photos of dramatic skin health improvement. So who needs your business the most? For example, if you're a freelance web designer, blue-collar business owners not known for their online presence could really use your services to boost their online presence.

❑ **2. Contact one or two people to demo your work: 15 minutes**

Maybe you can think of several people in your network who could get value from your product or service. Choose one or two people to contact. That's all you need. Then reach out with a simple offer—*You get my product/service at no cost to you, and I get to track your progress.*

❑ **3. Demo your product or service, capture before versus after proof, and ask for the sale: 30 minutes**

Let your one or two test subjects demo your product or service. Take before and after photos/screenshots so future customers can clearly see progress—progress worth paying for. For example, a web designer can take a picture of the plumber's website from 1998 and showcase it side by side with the new, beautiful, responsive design. The designer could then offer to design flyers and other marketing materials for a fee.

Like Rin, you can expect at least one person to accept your offer. And why not? You've already proven you know what you're doing. One of the biggest reasons new business owners like you don't get customers is people don't trust them because they have no track record to show. You're not even a month into the life of your business, and today you're handling a top objection to the sale. You'll benefit from your efforts today for the rest of your life.

Daily Standup

Did you complete today's tasks?

- ❑ Yes
- ❑ No

If no, what do you need to carry over to work on tomorrow?

____

What did you learn about your business (or yourself) today that will serve you in the future?

____

Day 28: Teach Customers to Buy from You

It Takes a Village to Build a Business

Dr. Michele Raithel is a doctor of naturopathic medicine, or ND. If you don't know what naturopathic medicine is, don't worry—you're not alone. Michele faced this lack of awareness about her profession when she started Revolutions Naturopathic in 2009. The first thing she needed to do was to educate the local population about naturopathic medicine. So I'd better start today's activities with an introduction as well.

Naturopathic medicine is a distinct primary health-care profession emphasizing prevention, treatment, and optimal health through the use of therapeutic methods and substances that encourage individuals' inherent self-healing process. Michele's husband Justin is now operations manager, but when she started the business, he worked as a petroleum engineer for a large multinational exploration and production company in North Africa. He took an assignment in Algeria where he worked for a month and then would come home for a month. When Justin got off work every day at 7:00 p.m., he took advantage of downtime and internet access to help with the database design and software development. Then when he came home, he had a month without work. No emails, no calls, nothing. For Justin, it felt like all the time in the world to help out his wife. Only when the business grew and needed more operational support did Justin join Revolutions Naturopathic full time.

How else is naturopathic medicine different from mainstream medicine? Well, at most doctors' offices, your medical care is billed to insurance. Insurance-based health-care companies set the amount of time patients can spend with their doctor. Revolutions Naturopathic offers a consultative model where patients can come in and spend as much time as they want with the doctor. They can run pretty much any lab tests they want and get the expertise of a doctor for as long as they want to ask as many questions as they want. Nowadays, people want that one-on-one attention. Most naturopathic businesses provide more time to patients, but some have set standard fees and standard appointment times. Revolutions Naturopathic doesn't. Dr. Michele Raithel has set an hourly rate, so it's like going to a CPA, attorney, or even a mechanic. Certain people don't need the education about whatever disease they have. They just want to get in and out with a treatment plan and some answers. Others want to learn about the biochemical process causing their body not to function correctly and go through all of their options. That personalized education helps them make the changes they need to get healthy again.

Dr. Michele Raithel doesn't believe in putting patients on a pharmaceutical that they need to get refilled every three to six months so she can keep getting paid. Most primary care in the United States is associated with people calling to make doctors' appointments so they can refill their prescriptions. At Revolutions Naturopathic, the desire is to get patients off prescriptions they don't need or to keep them from starting unnecessary prescriptions in the first place. So Michele doesn't have that hook that keeps people coming back forever. That's by design. She wants to make you feel better so that you improve and get back to life as you knew it. That gives Michele a business challenge—she has to constantly find new patients. Fortunately, her patients take care of that for her. They go and tell ten family members and friends how they've gotten off drugs or how they feel so much better. About half of all Revolutions Naturopathic patients show up through word-of-mouth referrals. Oftentimes, Mom comes in first because women take care of themselves much better than men. They're the gatekeeper for the family's health, so a couple of months later, the husband and kids become patients too. All it takes is one person to understand the power of naturopathic medicine for their entire network to become believers.

It wasn't this easy at the start of her business. As naturopathic medicine was not well established when Dr. Michele Raithel started, she first needed to educate her prospective clients about naturopathy. She worked extensively with her local Chamber of Commerce to educate the other alternative practitioners in the area like chiropractors, acupuncturists, and massage therapists. When these practitioners' patients heard about the new naturopathic clinic, they decided to give Michele a try. Soon Revolutions Naturopathic grew into two locations and eight doctors to become one of the largest naturopathic practices in the western United States. It all started with educating the community, including patients, other health-care professionals, and the Chamber of Commerce. Even if you're not a naturopathic doctor, you can teach people to buy from you. And it's not as hard as it sounds.

Educate Before You Market

This strategy takes time to get results, but the customers who come through this strategy will trust you more and stay with you longer. Depending on your business, that time could be as short as one month (online, consulting, coaching businesses) or longer for a brick-and-mortar business like Revolution Naturopathic. Here are a few tips to educate your prospects so that they become customers:

1. **Believe in your product or service:** First you must innovate enough to come up with a product or service that delivers exceptional value and believe in that.
2. **Express that belief:** There are many examples of companies that do this well. Think Apple, Nike, and Johnson & Johnson, to name a few.
3. **Leverage established thought leaders:** If nobody knows who you are or what your business offers, identify established thought leaders in related fields. Find a way to connect with them to get your message out.

Customer Education: Now It's Your Turn

Check off the box beside each task as you complete it.

❑ **1. Assess and document your prospective customers' awareness of your business: 15 minutes**

Does your target market know what you sell and why they need your product or service? If your answer to either question is a clear no, or if you're not sure, you have some educating to do.

❑ **2. Identify potential collaborators to work with to get your message out: 15 minutes**

What businesses does your target market buy from? How can you work together to promote each other's businesses? For example, you could offer to stock your product on a well-known store's shelves, and let the owner take a fair share of the profit. You can do the same with a service.

- ❑ **3. Craft your pitch to your collaborators to educate the customers: 30 minutes**

  So you know a small business owner or service professional who already works with your target market. Turn that knowledge into revenue—make an irresistible offer with little risk and much reward. For example, if you offer an alternative health and wellness service, you could offer your services to an established physical therapist's clientele. Pitch the therapist this idea—they tell their patients about your services via email, social media, mail, or all three, and they receive up to 25 percent of the revenue from each booked session with you. You don't have to offer 25 percent, but the idea is that your collaborator gets to say yes to pretty much free money while you get your first paying customers.

Daily Standup

Did you complete today's tasks?

❑ Yes

❑ No

If no, what do you need to carry over to work on tomorrow?

____

What did you learn about your business (or yourself) today that will serve you in the future?

____

Day 29: Trade Services for Experience

Trying Every Sales Strategy You Can Imagine

Larissa Lowthorp owns TimeJump Media, a full-service entertainment and technology agency. Larissa and her team provide branding, design, video production, and marketing campaigns of all types. Larissa helps clients strategize and define their brand presence, build their digital identity, and build relationships with their core audience. TimeJump Media also provides screenwriting, copyediting, video production, and web development services.

Was starting TimeJump always part of the plan? Yes, actually. Larissa always expected to be a business owner. Her parents were entrepreneurs, and it was a given that one day she would do the same. She thought this would come in the form of taking the reins of her parents' company, but life had different things in store.

Larissa started her first small businesses as an elementary school student. Beginning in the fifth grade, she designed and later sold handmade jewelry to friends and fellow students.

In middle school, after unsuccessfully campaigning to her parents for a raise in allowance, Larissa decided to take matters into her own hands and go into business for herself.

She hung up hand-drawn signs for housekeeping, babysitting, and dog-walking services at stores, the local library, and churches around her hometown. Each sign had pull tabs with her phone number. When Larissa was a university student, entrepreneurship became a necessity. She worked a full-time early childhood education job, but the paychecks didn't cover tuition, much less living expenses. So Larissa side hustled as a nanny for two families to make ends meet and fund classroom supplies. She was internet savvy, and eBay was the place to buy and sell vintage and secondhand products. Without a degree or much work experience, Larissa had the idea to turn her longtime thrifting and antiquing hobby into a profitable eBay business by digging through the Salvation Army toy bins, stopping by garage sales, and picking up and refurbishing discarded items on the side of the road. Most searches ended in dead ends. But Larissa had an intuitive understanding of kitsch items that could be marked up for a profit. For example, she found a 1980s My Little Pony at a thrift store for $1, which she sold for $80, and a mint-condition vintage Japanese doll she bought for $12.50 and sold for $325. That wasn't a lot of money, but those treasures got her by when she had no other options.

In order to increase awareness and drive online shoppers to her eBay store, Larissa built search-engine friendly websites and landing pages and marketed them via online message boards to build relationships and convert potential customers. It was all grassroots, but it had an impact. Larissa figured out what worked best as she went along. When she sold an item she purchased at a low cost, she watched for it on her next thrifting expeditions. She loved being the seller with that one thing that made customers happy. It brought her a lot of joy when customers would email her to say how an item she sold connected them to a special memory.

The library had a shelf where people could leave discarded books, and anybody could take them to keep for free. Larissa picked up an interesting-looking paperback about mermaids once. After she read it, she put it on eBay. This old paperback sold for a couple of hundred dollars. She asked her customer about it, and the buyer explained that it was a rare, out-of-print first edition. That's when Larissa got involved in selling rare and out-of-print books. She found a local used book shop that sold discarded books (sometimes in new condition) for a dollar or two each. She watched eBay auctions like a hawk to see which old books sold for the highest prices.

Now selling classic toys and hard-to-find books that were in high demand, Larissa soon became an eBay PowerSeller, an elite distinction reserved for stores that sell a high volume of products, sales with a dollar threshold per month, or both. PowerSellers must maintain exemplary customer service, customer satisfaction, and a high feedback rating.

Around this time, Larissa's parents fell on hard times. She dropped out of college and moved home. To make extra money, she pivoted her eBay business to vintage designer and luxury fashion. Her best find was a vintage $7 Louis Vuitton Damier wallet from a thrift store. She sold it on eBay for $400. As business picked up, she experimented with drop-shipping—listing items for sale and purchasing them from a third-party seller after a sale. The third-party vendor would ship the item directly to Larissa's customer. Larissa spent a lot of time building relationships and establishing trust with merchants and manufacturers in Asia and learning the ins and outs of doing business with offshore partners. She handled customer service and sales, which the vendor packaged and shipped. But Larissa learned too late that the drop-shipping market was oversaturated for many popular product categories, and not all vendors could be trusted. Items her customers ordered were out of stock, and she had to ask them to wait or refund their money. Worse, one supplier sent customers subpar-quality products—a bait-and-switch after Larissa hand-provided quality control on sample inventory and approved the product. Drop-shipping just wasn't sustainable. Larissa sold a lot, but profit margins were razor thin.

That's when Larissa decided to enter the corporate world, starting at the bottom, with the dream of working her way up to a higher income in order to save enough money to someday open Lowthorp Enterprises, the name she'd picked for her would-be conglomerate. A five-year plan, right? Excited about her new direction, Larissa dove into the job listings. She could build websites, so why not get a full-time web developer job? Except they all required experience and a four-year degree, neither of which Larissa had. If she could just land an interview, Larissa knew she had the creativity, drive, and know-how to do the job.

An advertising executive noticed Larissa's portfolio and recognized her talent. He decided to take a chance on her. Larissa began as an intern and moved up one role at a time. Corporate life let Larissa grow in a professional environment that complemented her previous bootstrapped business experience. Within a few years, Larissa got an offer for her dream job as an information architect, designer, and brand engineer, providing creative direction at one of the top twenty companies in the Fortune 500. However, after a couple of years, Larissa came to realize she'd given up everything she'd envisioned for life, and her plan to exit the corporate world and focus on her business and passion projects wasn't coming to fruition. She felt stuck. Larissa had taken a break from working with freelance clients to build her career. Step by step, sacrifice by sacrifice, Larissa had become successful, but at a tremendous cost. She'd set aside the business she hoped to build in exchange for comfort and security. Larissa felt guilty because she'd worked hard for everything she'd achieved, and she did not want to seem ungrateful. But she could no longer deny her dissatisfaction. The nine-to-five wasn't her anymore.

Finally, Larissa took action—she left her corporate job and took on consulting projects to pay bills and keep food on the table. It was worth it. So was all the hardship she faced. When a dear friend nudged Larissa to start her own media company, she finally made her dream come true. She incorporated TimeJump Media in October 2018 after its informal beginnings a year and a half prior. Finally, Larissa's tech knowledge and creative spirit converged in something amazing.

A Faster Way to Paying Customers: Trade Services for Experience

As with previous businesses, Larissa tried many marketing methods to get customers for TimeJump Media. Methods she'd become familiar with throughout her career included word of mouth, printed signs, banner ads, direct mail, cold calls, cold emails, social media marketing, and paid search marketing. Cold calls and emails didn't work at all. Direct mail was expensive and unproven. Larissa could never be certain who got her mail or whether they took an action like calling, contacting her, or visiting her website. Email blasts could end up classified as spam— even when users had asked to receive emails. Email marketing can be effective for certain demographics. Not Larissa's.

What about advertising? Larissa believes banner ads need to be strategically placed to get attention. She thinks of banner ads as more of a behavior prediction tool because they tell you what grabs audience interest. Use this information to direct future marketing campaigns.

Social media marketing has been good for TimeJump exposure and brand awareness, but not direct conversions. TimeJump offers bespoke services. Where social media can be of great value to a company such as Larissa's is not in sponsored or paid advertising but in forum posts and group engagements creating high-quality interactions that establish credibility and build trust. Companies in other industries may have different experiences with social media. If you're going to market on social media, you need to be savvy with it yourself or hire a company that can help you strategize.

Of everything Larissa tried to get clients, she found personal connections and conversations most effective. Larissa has a proven track record with people whom potential clients trust and whose opinion they value. For Larissa, referrals have brought her marketing, IT services, and web design clients. That said, she didn't find her first paying customer in her network. That first sale happened because of a trade. Here's the story:

Larissa's first web design customer was a photography studio. When she worked in corporate, one of her projects was to design the studio's website. But the client's project got sidelined. Larissa realized that working one on one with this studio would not violate her employer's noncompete agreement, and after verifying with her employer, she reached back out to the studio and offered to finish the website for free in exchange for professional headshots.

This technique worked—with the studio and with future customers. In the early days of Larissa's freelance business, she tried it with everyone she encountered. When she visited a shop, she'd ask the owner if they had an online presence. If the store sold something she couldn't afford, Larissa asked the owner if they'd trade a product for a website. Many said yes. These first web design clients soon sent referrals to real paying customers, who in turn referred more business. Larissa's revenue snowballed from there. Her first paying client was a website referral from a service exchange she did with a celebrity hairstylist. As Larissa's word-of-mouth referrals and reputation have grown, so has her client base. This strategy provided the foundations for TimeJump Media's subsequent success.

Trading Services Strategy: Now It's Your Turn

Check off the box beside each task as you complete it.

- ❑ **1. Identify potential partners for trading services: 20 minutes**

  What services would help you grow your business that you can't afford right now? Who do you know who offers these? Is there a chance—any chance at all—that these people might benefit from your product or service? List ten such business owners you might trade services with. Be sure to include people on your list who are well known or well liked in your city or industry so you'll get referrals to paying customers ASAP. That said, remember that referrals should always be earned. They are a privilege, not a right.

- [ ] **2. Craft your message: 40 minutes**

Reach out to potential partners via email. Use the template below to connect with ten potential partners. For this strategy to be effective, find something common like a mutual friend, a community service organization you both volunteer at, a Chamber of Commerce membership, et cetera. Here is one email template to use in your outreach.

Hi, [prospect's name],

I'm [your name] from [your company/brand name]. At the recent Chamber of Commerce outreach event, [name of mutual contact] told me about [your business/services] and the [project, if applicable] that you are currently working on. It's an awesome project that I can relate to because my business focuses on those services.

We have already done similar work, and you can check out the following links.

- [customer link, if available]
- [internal link, if no customer project testimonial is available]

I would be interested in completing the [project mentioned above] for no cost in exchange for [whatever the business can offer, like a photography session].

If you are interested, can we get on the phone and have a quick 10-minute call on [date and time] to discuss the specifics?

Regards,

[your name and contact info]

You get the idea. Try to find as much common ground as possible. The ultimate goal is that this nonpaying customer will either refer paying customers or become a paying customer in the future.

Daily Standup

Did you complete today's tasks?

- ❑ Yes
- ❑ No

If no, what do you need to carry over to work on tomorrow?

____

What did you learn about your business (or yourself) today that will serve you in the future?

____

Day 30 How Passionate Are You?

First Paying Customer at Fifteen Years Old

Rob Ross has been passionate about computers since he was a teenager. When he was thirteen, he began working at a local computer store doing odd jobs and helping customers. By fifteen, he was confident enough to start his own computer business by importing computers and parts from Taiwan. Rob signed a commercial lease for an office space, which became the home of his first company, RLR Systems Plus.

Within a year of forming RLR Systems Plus, Rob was able to purchase a computer company from a friend who worked at Hewlett-Packard. He merged the new company into RLR Systems Plus. Rob discovered he had an uncanny ability to identify tech industry trends and was able to ride the upside of these trends. Within three years, he sold RLR Systems Plus.

Now what? Well, Rob loved technology and business and was hooked. In 1988, he launched his second company, Integral Networking Corporation. This company focused on remotely managing customers' computer servers and networks. At that time, most small-to-medium-size companies found it difficult to manage computer infrastructure that was usually spread out over multiple locations. Integral Networking's service offering solved this pain point, so his company thrived. Rob grew Integral Network and (fortuitously) sold it in 1999 to a San Francisco–based internet company that was completing an IPO. Then the internet bubble burst, and the technology industry crashed.

Once the dust settled a year later, Rob took on yet another passion project. He started and incorporated Think Smart Group Inc, where he remains as the president and majority owner. Rob took what he learned from Integral Networking and offered a better way to manage client's computer networks remotely. While successful, Rob spotted an emerging market opportunity in hosting vertical market applications in the cloud. Rob pivoted Think Smart to offer this service as well. Like Amazon Web Services and Microsoft Azure Cloud, Think Smart hosts non-web-based vertical market applications in the cloud, essentially providing access to those critical apps from anywhere via the web.

Hosting and supporting these applications for clients made Think Smart a one-stop shop where clients no longer needed an on-site server to run their business. They could simply focus on their business instead of worrying about technology management.

Rob locates his customers by working with software companies that make applications that run a specific type of business and require the client to have a server. Think Smart works with that software company to "web enable" their applications and offer their clients hosting and support, which becomes a win for both the software vendor and the customers. Think Smart has found a home in the health-care industry, currently serving both optometry and dentistry markets. Think Smart is currently the largest cloud provider for optometrists with customers in all fifty states.

Rob attributes a large part of his business success to his passion. Rob has always loved using computers to make life easier. Rob's first customer saw his passion for computers, believed in him, and gave Rob his first computer order. It was Rob's passion for technology that led him to start his first, then second, then third company. Today Rob believes in "paying it forward" and often consults and works with startups that show passion in their chosen field, helping them avoid the common pitfalls in starting a company.

So, what are you passionate about? Your passion may not be managed cloud services like Rob's, but if you're going to "make it" at Rob's level, finding a passion that pushes you to succeed—and pulls customers to you—is key.

Passion Alone Can Attract Customers

Passion is one of the most important ingredients of any successful business. In this chapter, you're going to use your passion as a strategy to get paying customers. When you're passionate about your business, you become more confident. That confidence pulls prospects toward you. Even if your offer isn't the cheapest or the fastest, you'll have the best presentation.

In general, customers who patronize small businesses do so because they've bought into the vision and passion of the business owner. Sure, the product or service has to solve a pain point for the customer, but their decision to purchase from you (rather than from your competitor) is often motivated by the passion you show for your business.

I already know you're passionate about starting and building your own business. How do I know that? First, you bought this book. Second, you found time to read it. So how will you show your passion for what you believe in to your potential customers? Your every action should convey your conviction and passion to your customers, whether it's via email, a phone call, or a face-to-face meeting. Passion isn't something you can fake—your customers will see right through you. You must truly believe in your business, your products and services, and yourself.

Every prospect you talk to should be drawn to your passion. *Wow, this person is so excited about what they do! Now I'm excited too!* In today's hyperconnected, overstimulated world, people get bored. Walk into any fast-casual restaurant during workweek lunch hour, and you'll see people staring off into space or staring at their smartphones. Blank looks. Very little "life." *You* can be the one who changes that for your customers. Like *The Wizard of Oz*, you and your business can bring beauty and color to an otherwise drab, black-and-white world.

Most entrepreneurship books tell you to "start with why." I'm telling you to *end* with why. Now that you have fifteen different strategies to get your first paying customers, you've either landed your first customer or you're in talks with a prospect who will become your first customer. At this early stage of your business, your passion—why you're doing this—will carry your business forward. Without passion for what you're doing, you won't pursue that second customer, the third, and beyond. Because it won't always be easy. But if you know why you're building this business and not any other, you will develop confidence you never knew was possible. That confidence will have paying customers rolling through your door.

Strategic Passion: Now It's Your Turn

Check off the box beside each task as you complete it.

❑ **1. Why are you passionate about this business?: 15 minutes**

Why did you decide to start this business? What do you love about it? Spend a few moments to write down why you're passionate about your business. It doesn't have to be fancy—just truthful.

- ❑ **2. List different ways you can express your passion: 30 minutes**

  Using what you wrote down in step one, think about how you can express your passion to your customers. Do you have an "origin story" that tells how you transformed yourself using the same product or service you're selling? If so, tell that story without holding back emotion. Does your product or service delight you? Then let customers see you smile. Whatever form your passion takes, it should do exactly that—take form. Write down three to five ways to express your passion about your business.

- ❑ **3. Communicate your passion: 15 minutes**

  How can you incorporate those expressions of passion into the daily operations of your business? Your passion should show up everywhere in your business—on your website, during your OPA presentation, in conversations, et cetera. Whether that's telling your origin story in a marketing email or simply smiling when you talk about your offer's features and benefits to a potential customer or employee, you want to communicate your passion in every aspect of your business. Write down three to five ways to communicate your expressions of passion about your business.

Daily Standup

Did you complete today's tasks?

- ❑ Yes
- ❑ No

If no, what do you need to carry over to work on tomorrow?

____

What did you learn about your business (or yourself) today that will serve you in the future?

____

The Finish Line (Or Is It?)

Whew! Congratulations. You have just crossed the thirty-day marathon finish line after sprinting daily for sixty minutes. That is an accomplishment worth celebrating.

If you have just been reading the book first to understand the concepts before actually implementing, congratulations are still in order for going over all the key concepts of the Agile Entrepreneur's way to start a business in thirty days or less and get paying customers.

If you have implemented the strategies mentioned in the book for the past month or so, you are most likely looking at one of the following three scenarios.

- **Scenario 1:** You've launched your business (as mentioned in the first fifteen days) and now have at least one paying customer thanks to the strategies covered on Days 16 through 30.
- **Scenario 2:** You launched your business (as mentioned in the first fifteen days) and tried your hand at a few marketing strategies but haven't succeeded yet. You're still waiting for that elusive first customer.
- **Scenario 3:** You were unable to launch your business because of some unexpected roadblocks you encountered.

For all three scenarios, the journey doesn't end here. There are multiple turns you can (and will) take to continue on your current path. If scenario 1 is your story, you have made a great accomplishment. You've overcome the most significant hurdle any entrepreneur will face—getting that first paying customer. Now your task is to go after the next set of customers. The same marketing methods you read on Days 16 through 30 will help you add to your revenue, then multiply it going forward. The most important strategy is customer referral generation from existing customers. Ask for testimonials and referrals, and don't be shy about it.

For scenario 2, your next key task is to learn from what failed. Which day's activities didn't pan out? Which strategy went wrong? Why? Many times, the strategy itself may not be the problem; it may simply need a little bit more time to work. Could that be the case in your situation? Or do you need to focus on other strategies mentioned in the book that you didn't get the chance to implement? Or both? In either case, reflect on your journey with a positive attitude. You now have a business that you can call your own. Use that reality to your advantage to promote your business in ways that you *know* work for other entrepreneurs just like you.

If scenario 3 best describes your situation, then you, my friend, have the easiest problem to fix. If you were unable to launch your business, more than likely the cause was inadequate resources. Not enough time, no money, not the right skills. So let's first figure out the underlying cause of why you didn't launch your business. Can you fix that issue? If you didn't have enough time, do you think you can find time in your schedule to go back and do the activities you skipped? If money was the problem, are you in a position to shore up finances without going broke? If it's a missing skill set, can you outsource or otherwise get help from family or friends to fill that gap? Perhaps someone you know who has the skills your business needs is thinking about starting a business. In that case, the simple solution that changes everything for you might be a partnership (Day 7).

The entrepreneurial journey is exhilarating and exhausting at the same time. Many veteran entrepreneurs will admit that the happiest and most depressing times of their lives have been during their business journey. Sometimes both at the same time. My effort with this book is to give this journey more balance. I want you to focus only on activities that lead to paying customers. After all, that is the only goal of a business, as Peter Drucker said. Rid yourself of all other noises. Keep asking yourself what innovation and what marketing you could do to create your next paying customer.

And if you need help, I am just one website away at www.The60MinuteStartup.com. If you have any questions, feel free to reach out to me at Contact@The60MinuteStartup.com. I promise to respond to you as soon as I can. (You can connect with me on LinkedIn as well.)

Thank you for reading *The 60-Minute Startup*, and congratulations on reaching this far. Your exhilarating journey has only begun.

Acknowledgments

Writing a book is an all-encompassing, time-consuming project but extremely gratifying. I am thankful to so many people who have helped shape my thoughts and have inspired me with their accomplishments. *The 60-Minute Startup* is now a reality thanks to you.

I want to thank all of the featured entrepreneurs in this book who opened up and shared their entrepreneurial journey with me. This book wouldn't have come alive without their personal stories.

I want to thank Jill Dyche who has enthusiastically supported my writing all along and was gracious enough to write foreword to this book

I want to express my gratitude to Joshua Lisec, who has been the "X factor" in this book project. He was my writing partner, guide, and editor of this book. I also want to acknowledge Joshua for coming up with the book title *The 60-Minute Startup*.

I want to thank Ali Saif, who has been my technology partner with www.RameshDontha.com and has helped me launch The Agile Entrepreneur Podcast in record time, ultimately inspiring this book.

I want to thank all my friends at Folsom Rotary, especially Rob Ross and Justin Raithel for encouraging me in all my endeavors.

Finally and most importantly, I want to thank my family, starting with my wife Sunanda for accepting all my crazy ideas, encouraging me, and allowing me to explore the uncharted territories. I immensely thank our two daughters, Megha and Nidhi, for helping me become a better parent, for constantly motivating me, and for all their contributions to making this book a reality.

About the Author

Ramesh Dontha is a serial entrepreneur, host of The Agile Entrepreneur Podcast, and author of *The 60-Minute Startup: A Proven System to Start Your Business in 1 Hour a Day and Get Your First Paying Customers in 30 Days* (or Less). As a manager and consultant for Fortune 100 companies, Ramesh used the agile methodology to make technology systems more efficient. He then applied agile principles to entrepreneurship, starting, growing, and selling multiple online businesses. Now Ramesh teaches aspiring entrepreneurs how to get paying customers faster than they ever thought possible. Start your business in sixty minutes a day at www.The60MinuteStartup.com.